I'll tell YOU a STORY

Photos & Stories

CATHRYN WELLNER

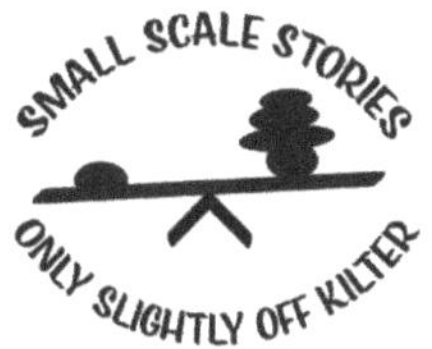

Small Scale Stories #7
Espoir Press
British Columbia 2017

Espoir Press
1002 - 1128 Sunset Drive
Kelowna, British Columbia
Canada V1Y 9W7

©2017 Cathryn Wellner

I'll Tell You a Story (Small Scale Stories #7)

978-1-988760-10-0

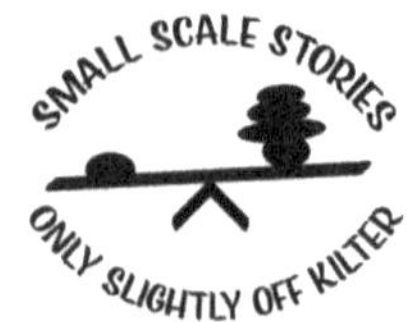

STORYTELLERS ARE EVERYWHERE

If we want to change something, we have to change the stories we tell about it. So this is a good time to talk about changing the stories we tell about this amazing planet and all that's on it. It's easy to do.

Sit at a wooden desk, and think about the tree it came from. Smell a flower, and consider what it would be like to spend all your life tethered to the earth. Watch a goose hanging out solo with a pair of mallards, and consider what made them companions. Duck for cover when a red-winged blackbird dive bombs your hair, and ponder what it must be like to be able to scare off birds many times your size.

Storytellers are everywhere. Sometimes they tell their stories with words. Other times they evoke them with a turn of the head, a funny dance, or a wild blossoming in a starkly ugly place. All we have to do is pay attention, ponder, and ask what role we play in changing the stories.

You are a storyteller. Everyone is. Be a storyteller for change, for honoring the earth, for loving the planet.

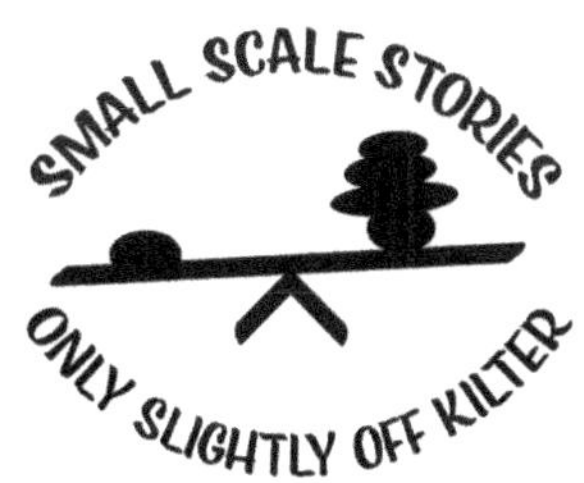

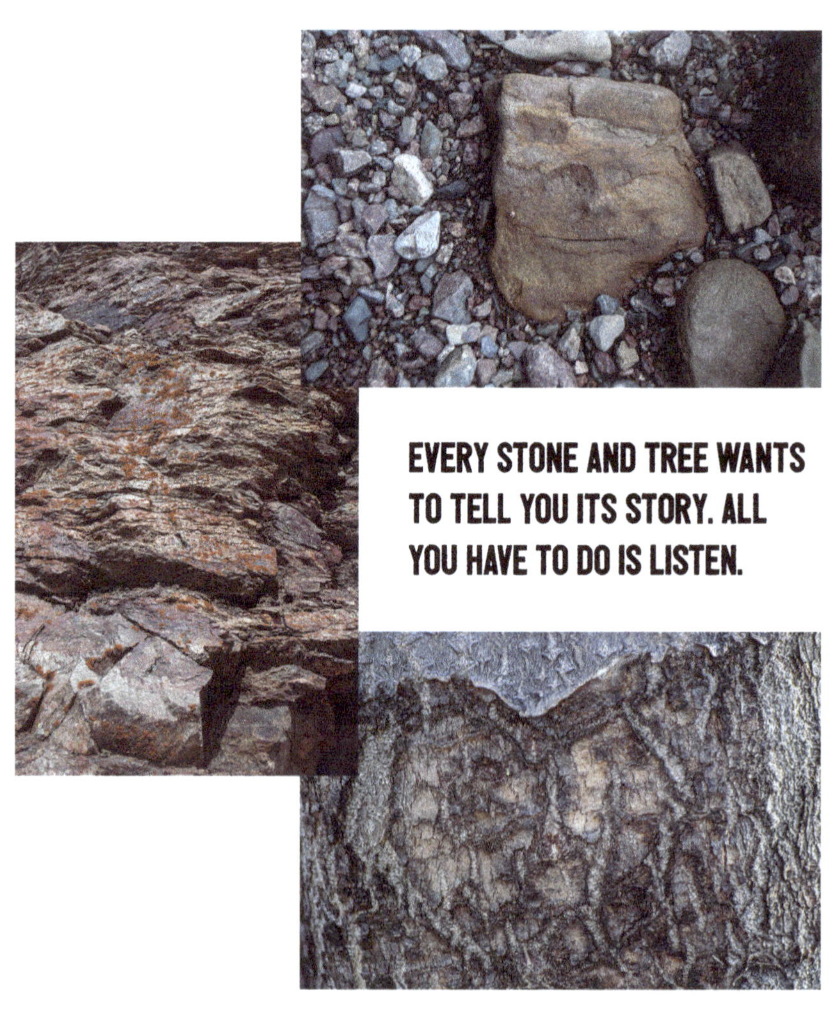
EVERY STONE AND TREE WANTS
TO TELL YOU ITS STORY. ALL
YOU HAVE TO DO IS LISTEN.

Stories are waiting

for your open heart

THE STORIES

1 Beach Stories
2 Alphabet Clouds
3 Freeing Her Roots
4 Angel Cloud
5 Best Friends
6 Circus Dreams
7 Cloud Games
8 Startling And Fun
9 Fashion Statement
10 Goldeneye's Dream
11 Hollyhocks
12 Hens' Rest
13 Jilted Merganser
14 Introvert Goose
15 Last Journey
16 Lift Up My Petals
17 Magic Pyramid
18 Predator Ball
19 Making Life Count
20 Repulsive Species
21 Queen Mallard
22 RWB's Good Day
23 Quiet Turtle
24 Shy Primrose
25 Remember The Farters
26 Yearning for Adventure
27 Shiny Muskrat
28 Silly Humans
29 Warm Time Solitude
30 Strange Habits
31 Snakes and Ladders
32 Something to Tell You
33 Tulip Trio
34 Tasty Daisy
35 Weary Travelers
36 Kindly Abelardo

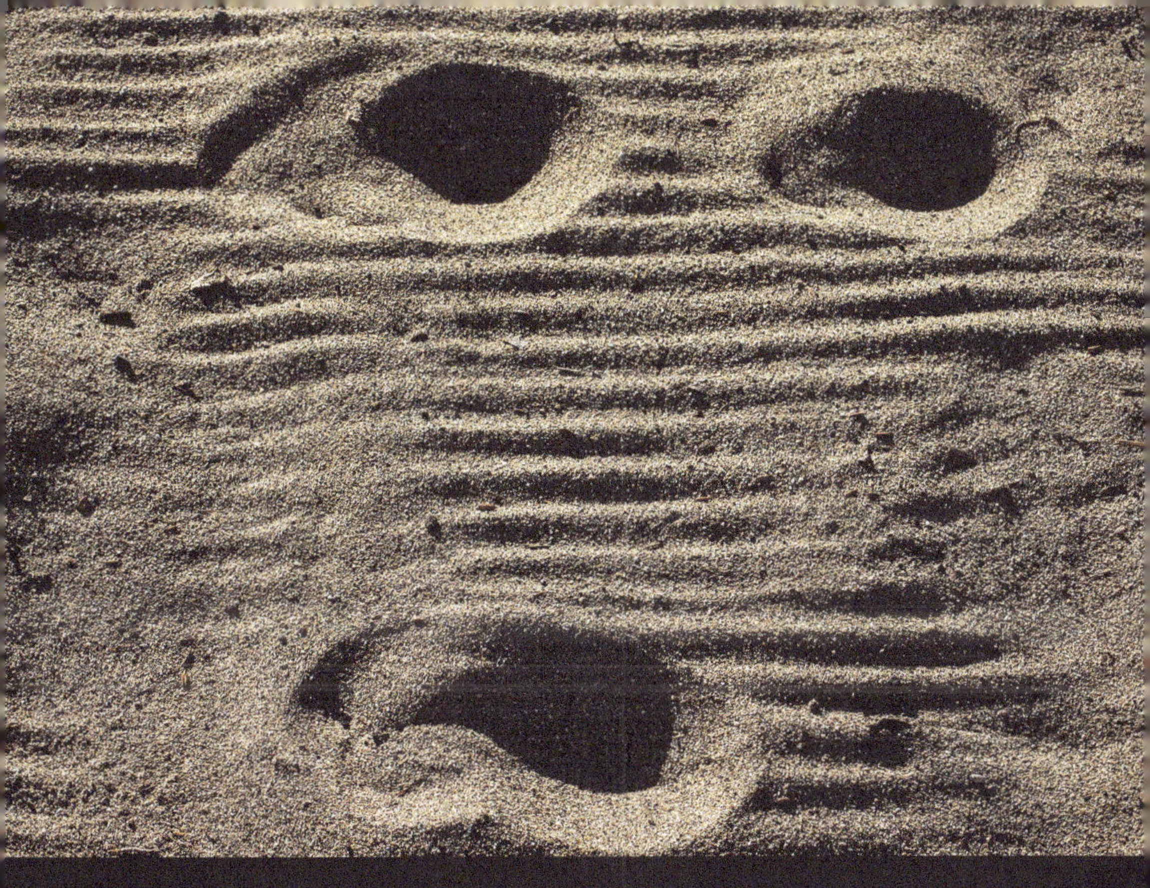

"Thanks for asking," said Sand. "Most people don't care we are gazillions of tiny pebbles. Some of us were mountains. Others were shells. We tell great travel stories. Do you mind if some of our tales are a bit...off color?"

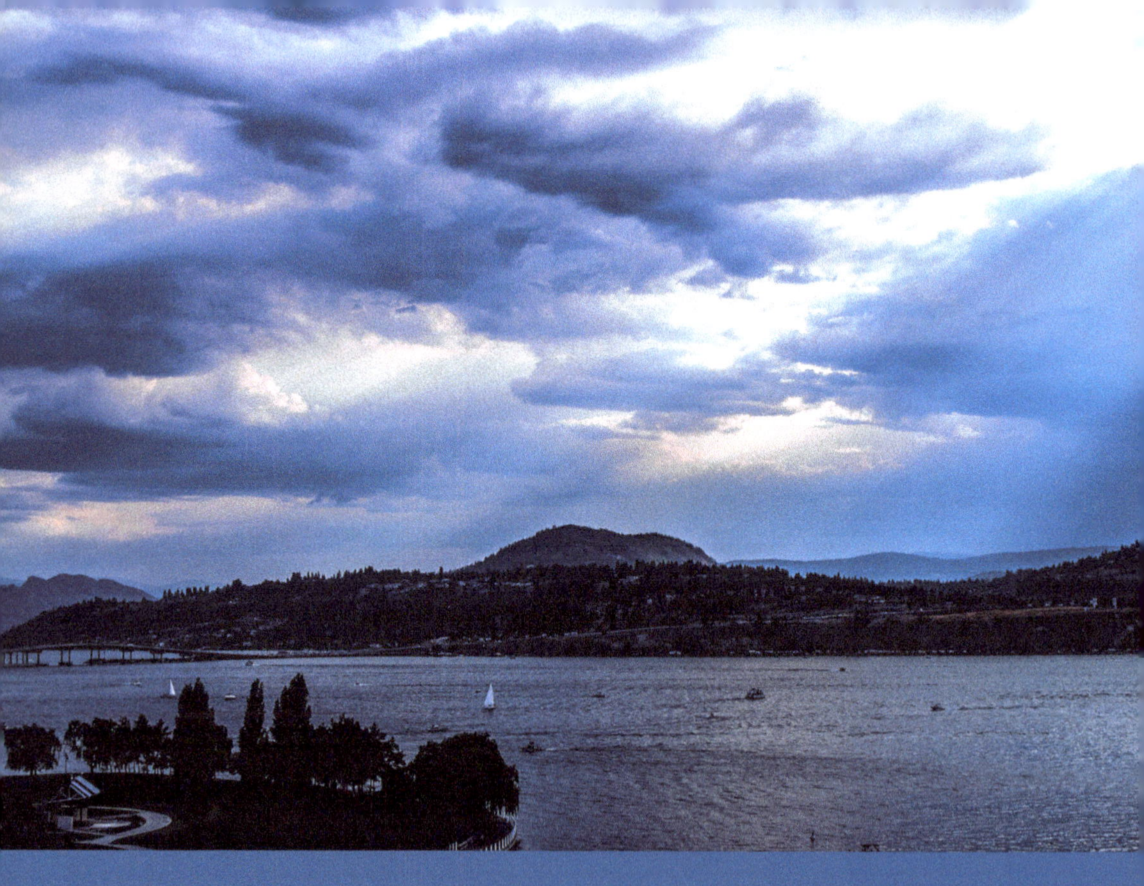

V Cloud called for partners for a game of Alphabets. When she accidentally bumped into W Cloud, he morphed into a seagull. That shifted the whole game. Nobody minded. Play was the point, not perfection.

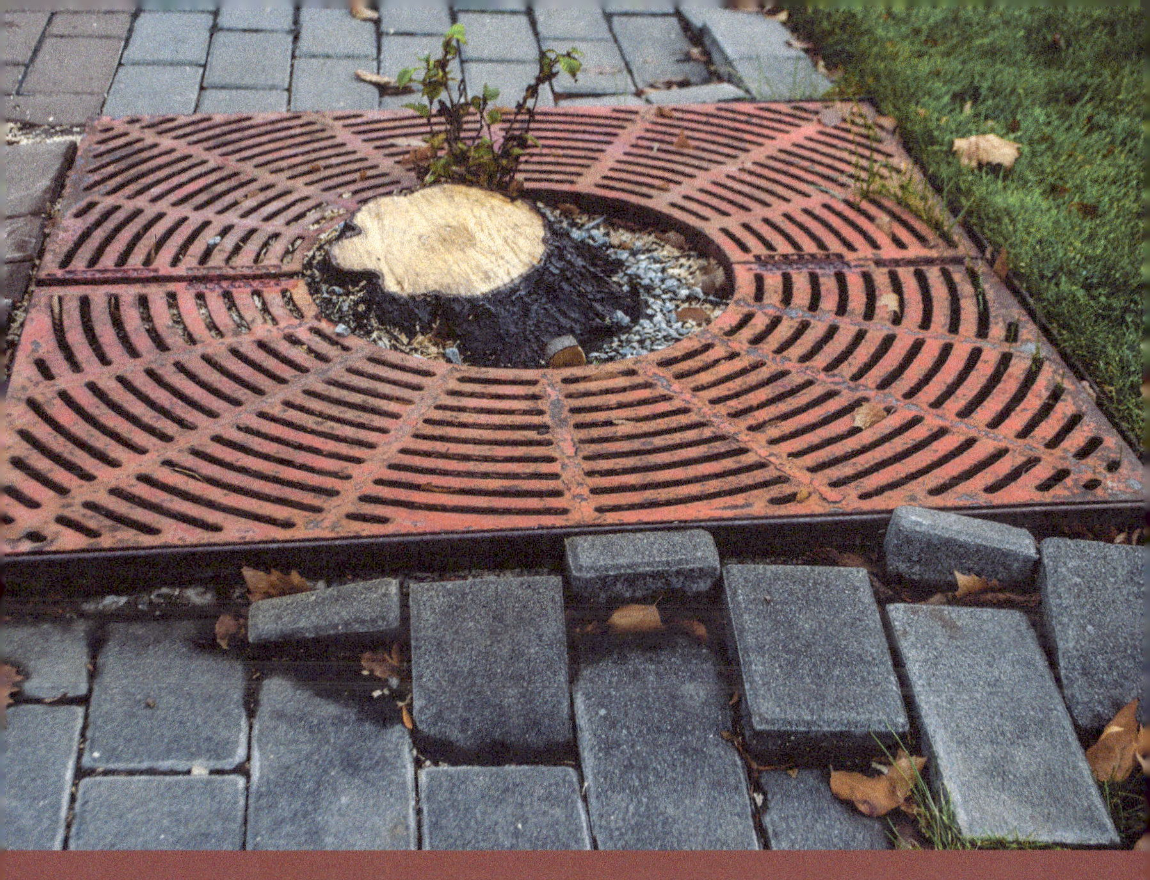

Tree pushed up the bricks bothering her roots.
Ah, it felt good to breathe more freely.
Unfortunately, some humans were not impressed
with her initiative.

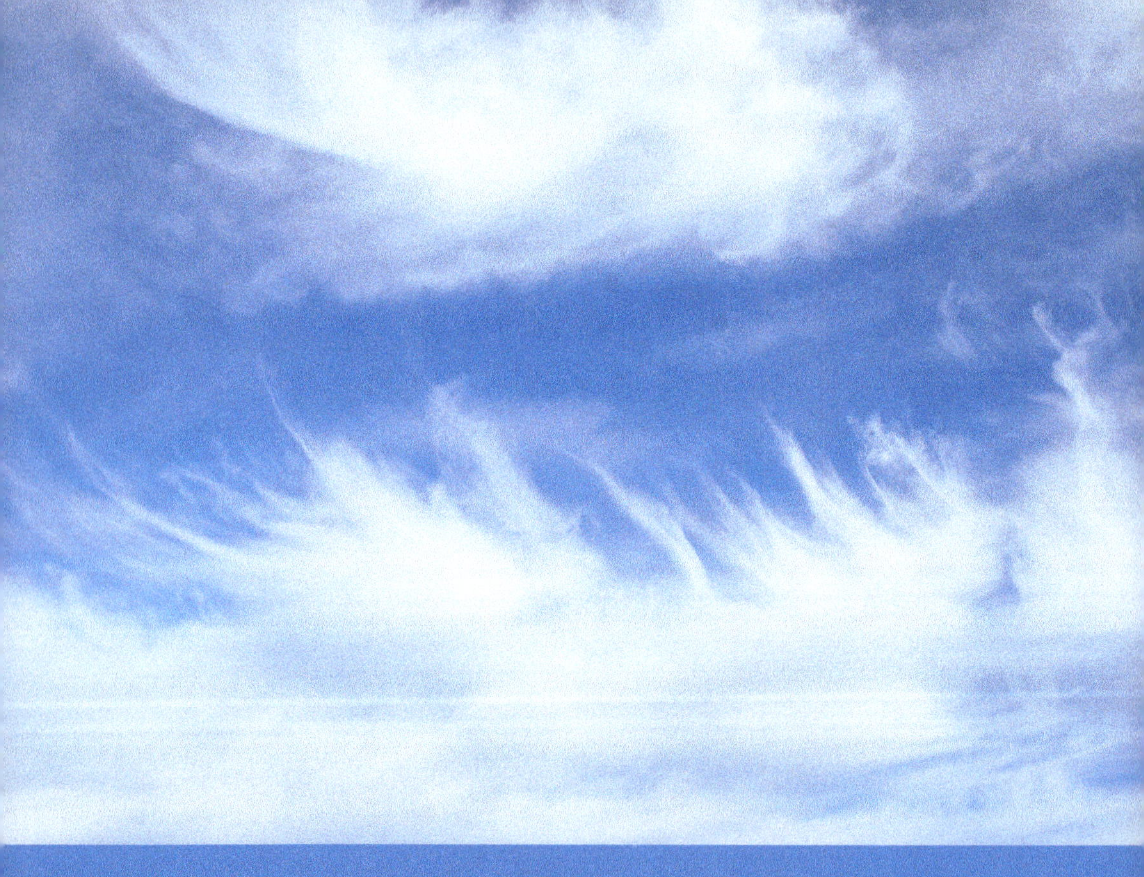

When Angel Cloud floated overhead, the clouds below reached up with feathery arms, hoping to touch her as she passed by.

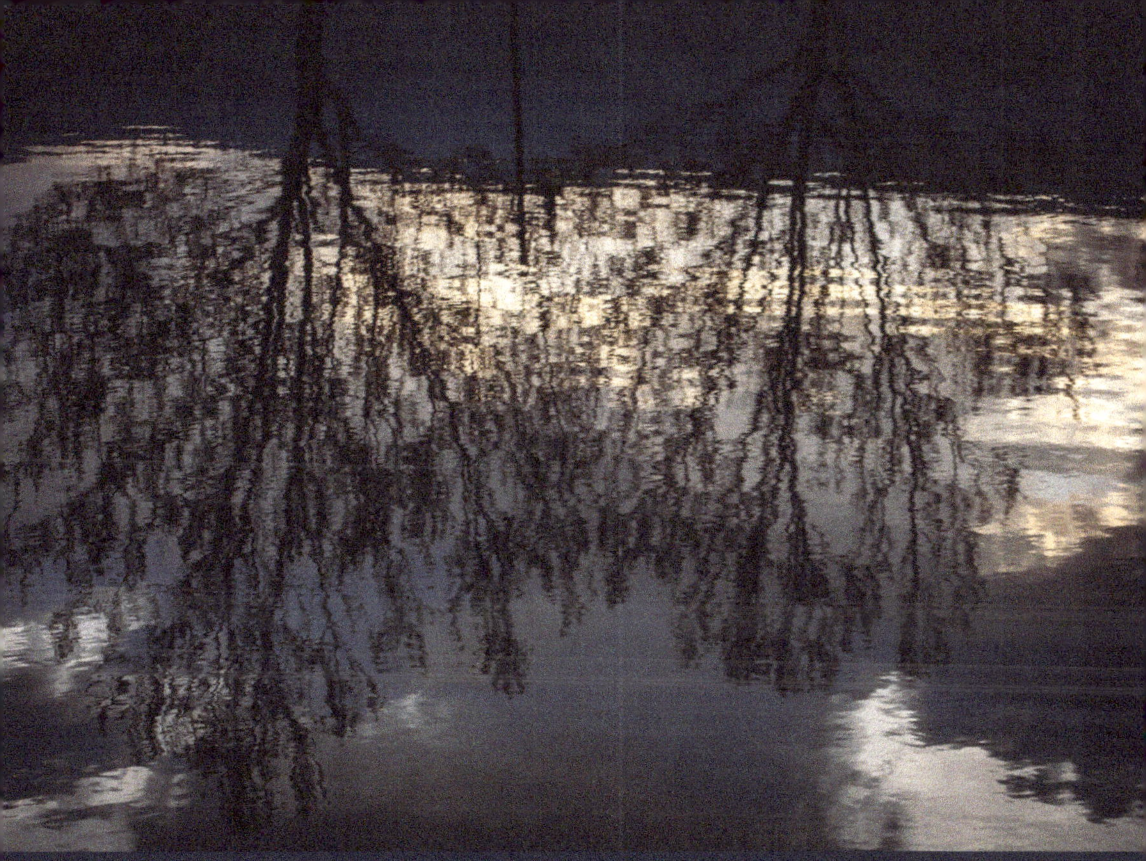

Standing side by side in the setting sun, the Tree Sisters looked down at their reflection. Their limbs were intertwined. Their roots connected beneath the grass. They were best friends in every way.

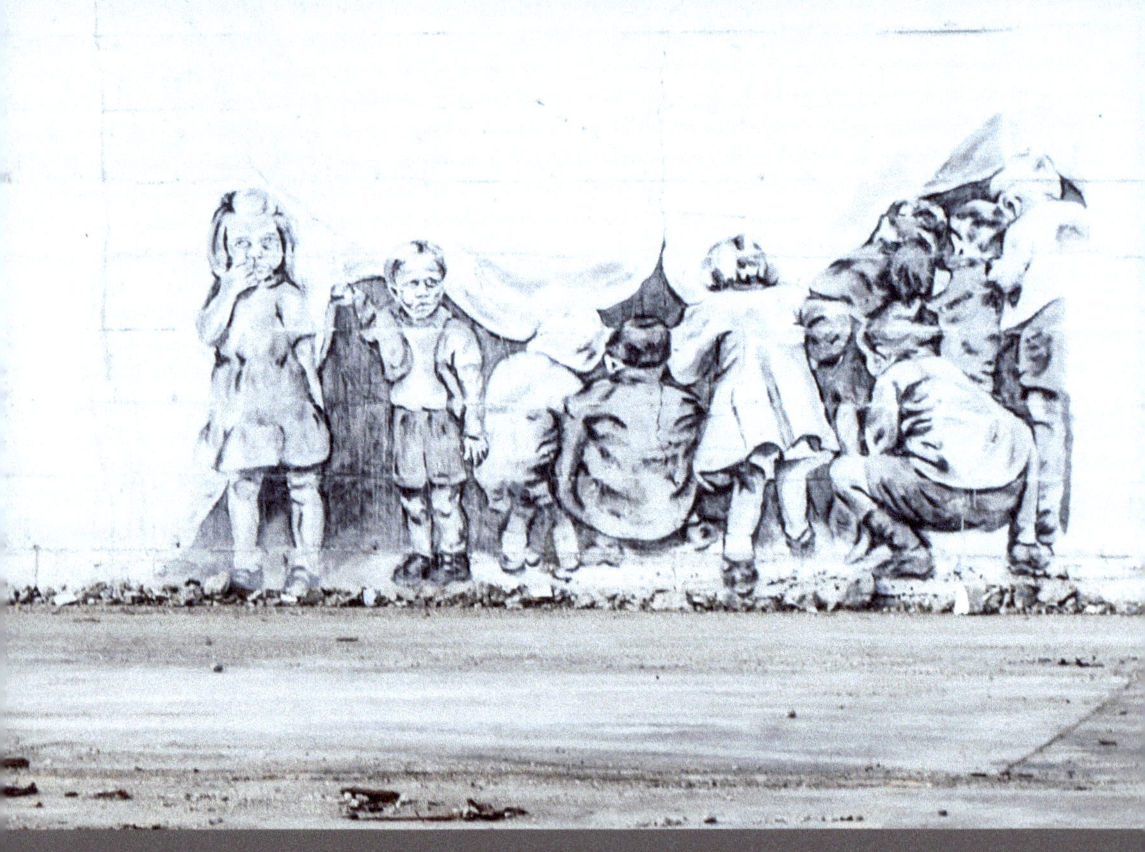

After years of trying to peek under the Big Tent to watch the circus, the children heard loud noises. They had no idea a demolition backhoe was about to end their circus dreams forever.

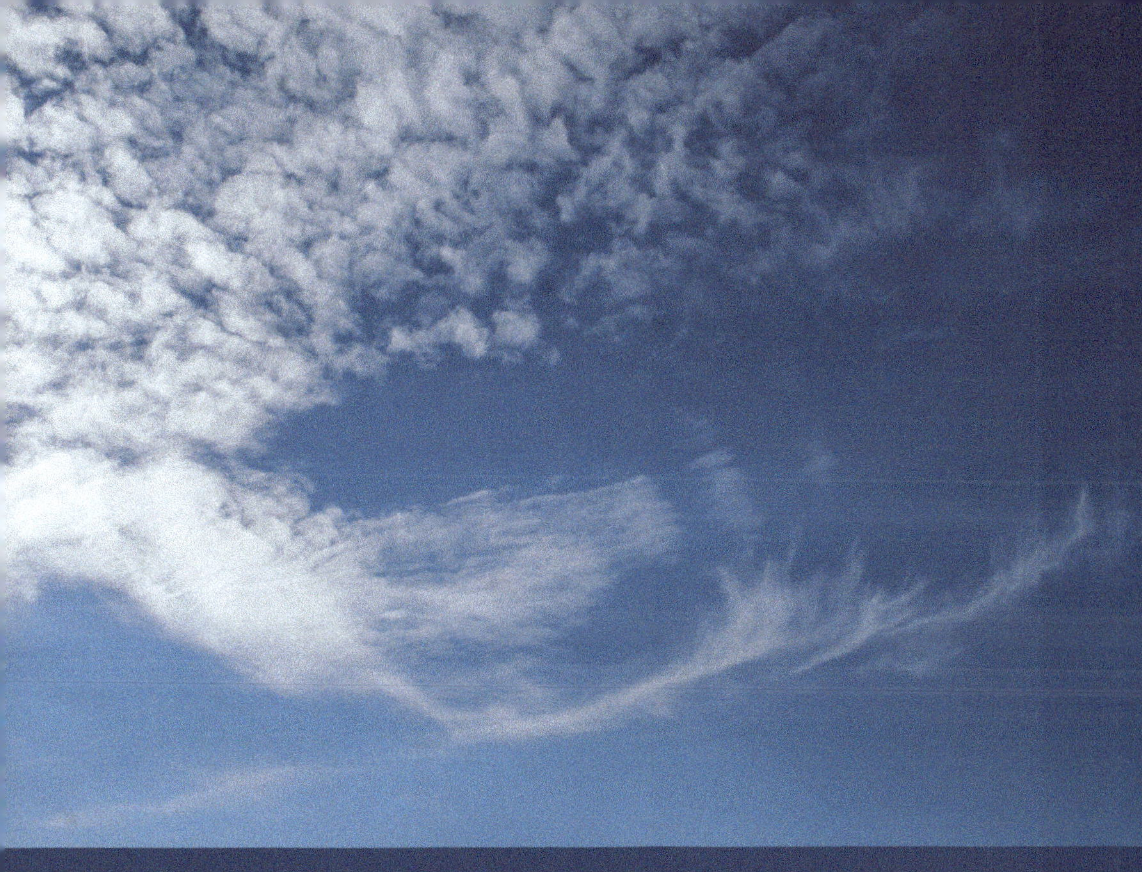

Cloud was trying to play the Bony Finger game.
Today she could not bring all the pieces together
so she experimented with a baby in a pea pod and
a chicken leg with feathers.

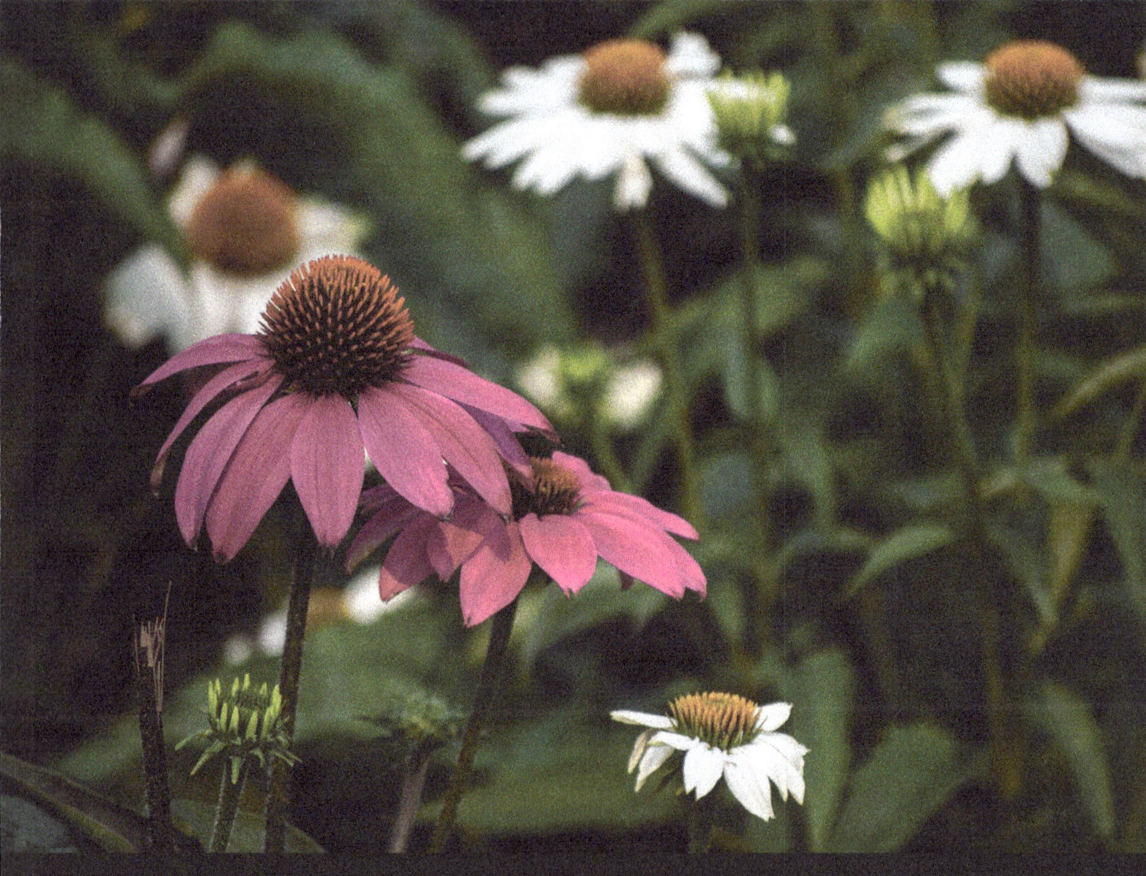

The gardener planned an all-white garden. Down the middle he planted a triangle of white coneflowers, with daisies around them. Another gardener with a sense of fun slipped in a pink coneflower. The effect was startling and fun.

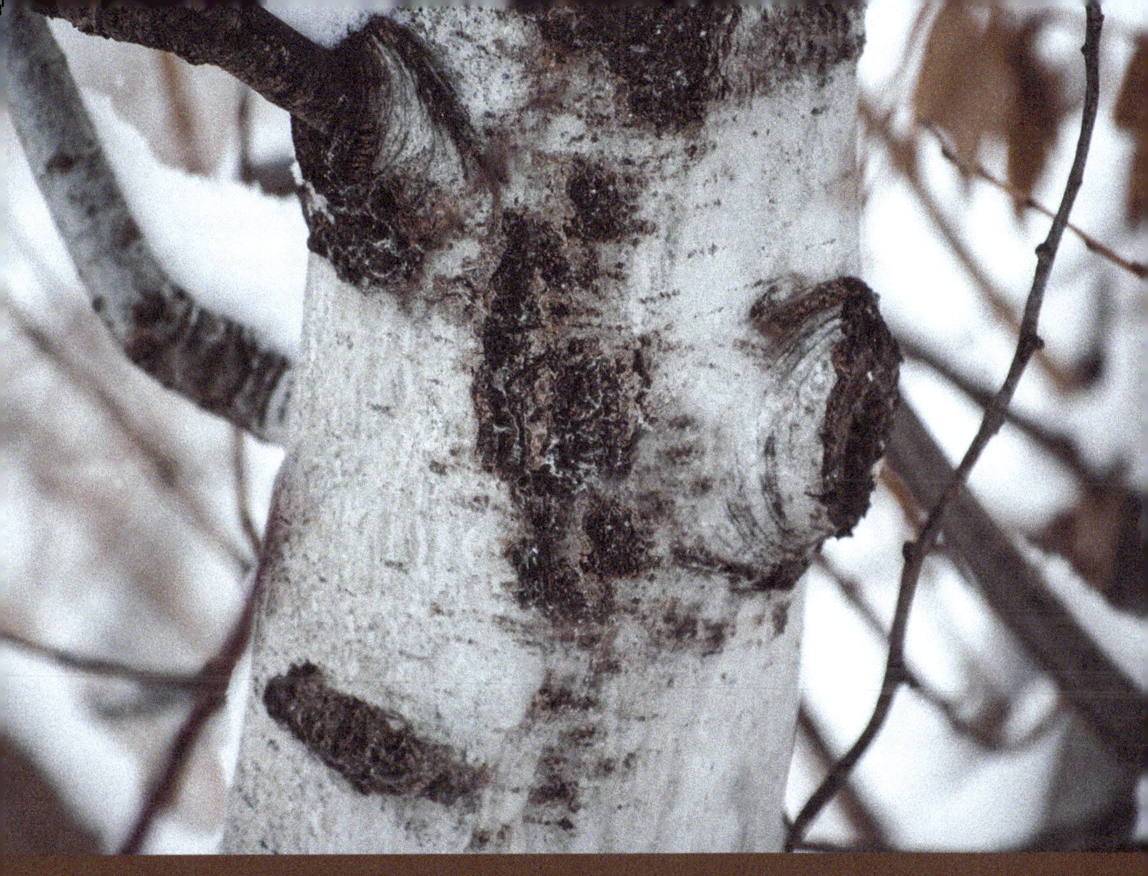

Tree knew she was making a fashion statement. Leaves clinging to her twigs matched the color on her trunk. She was amazed when only one person stopped to take a photograph.

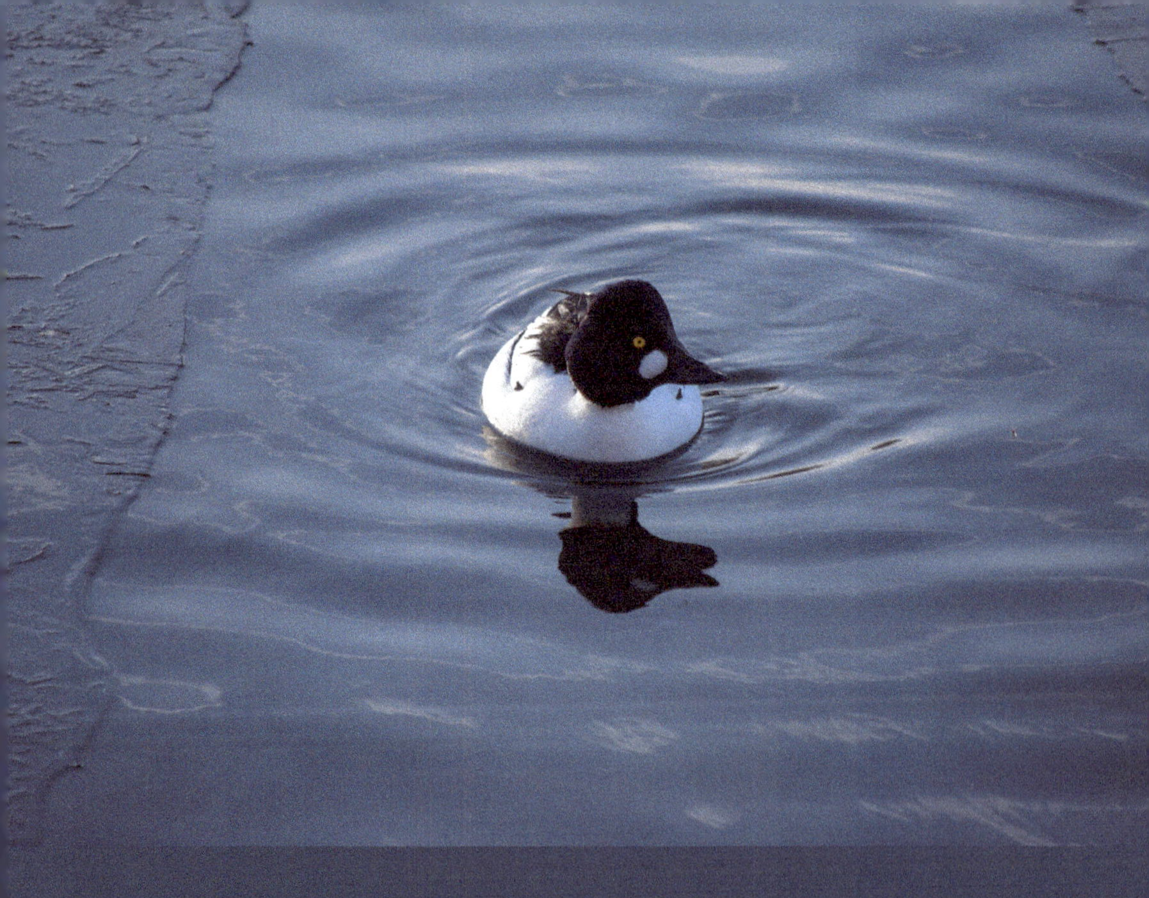

Goldeneye swam away from the ice. He was weary of winter. He dreamed of the season that led to happy mates and scrappy chicks.

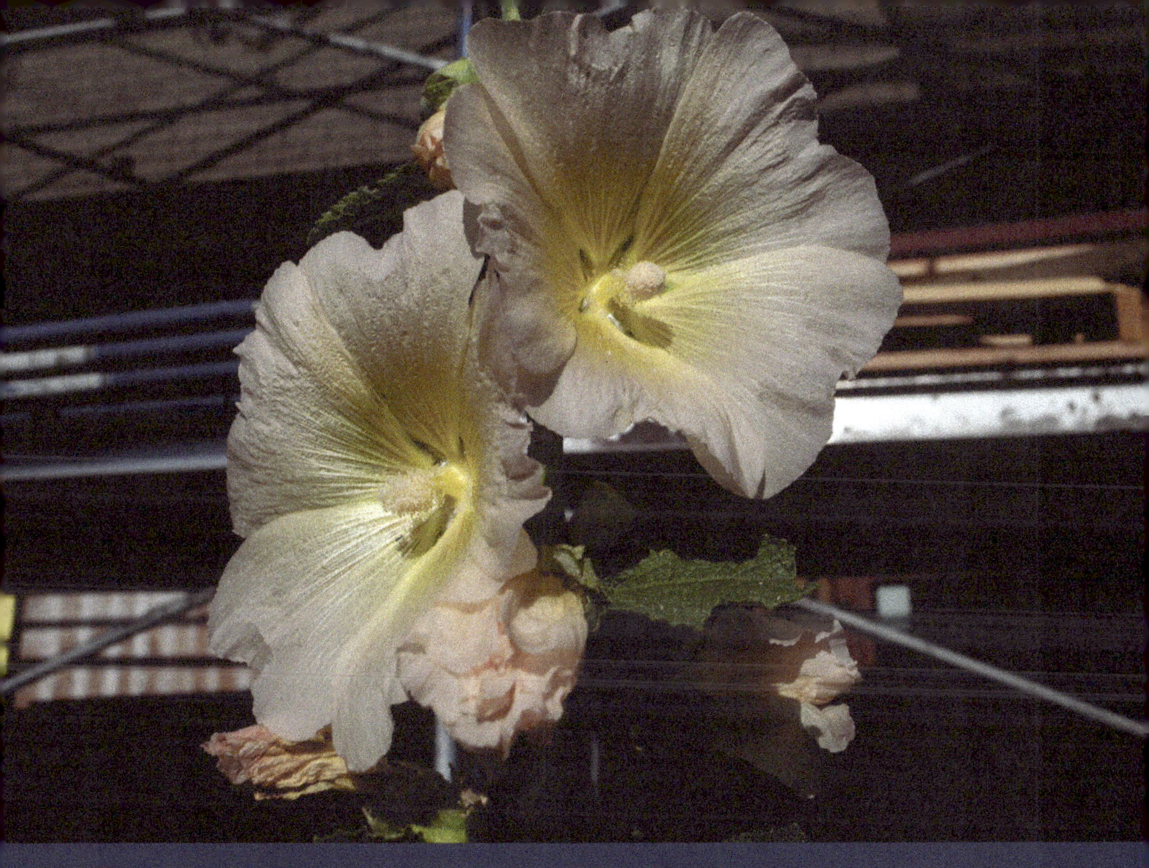

Hollyhocks grew in wild profusion between a parking lot and a construction site. The nearby streets were drab, but passersby caught sight of the flowers and found themselves smiling.

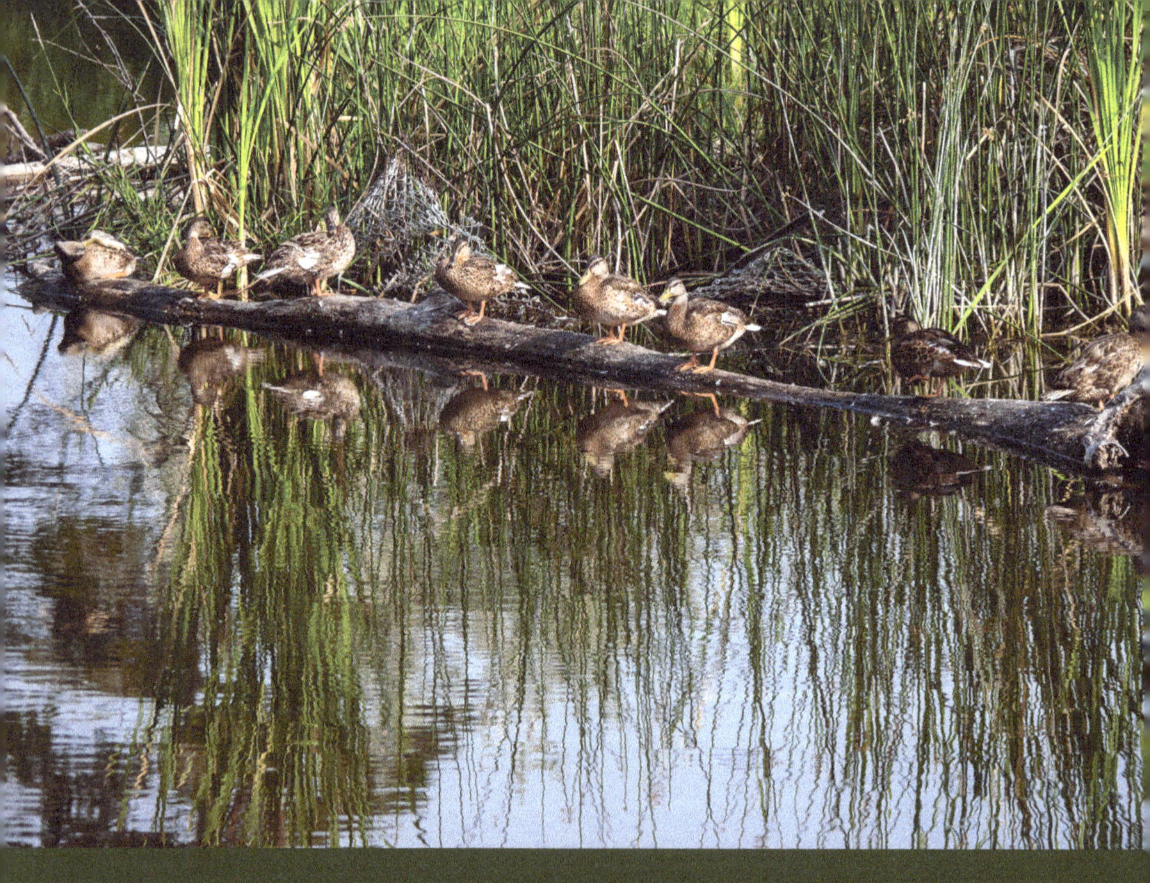

The mallard hens were peaceful. With the drakes off quacking and boasting, nothing disturbed the hens' rest.

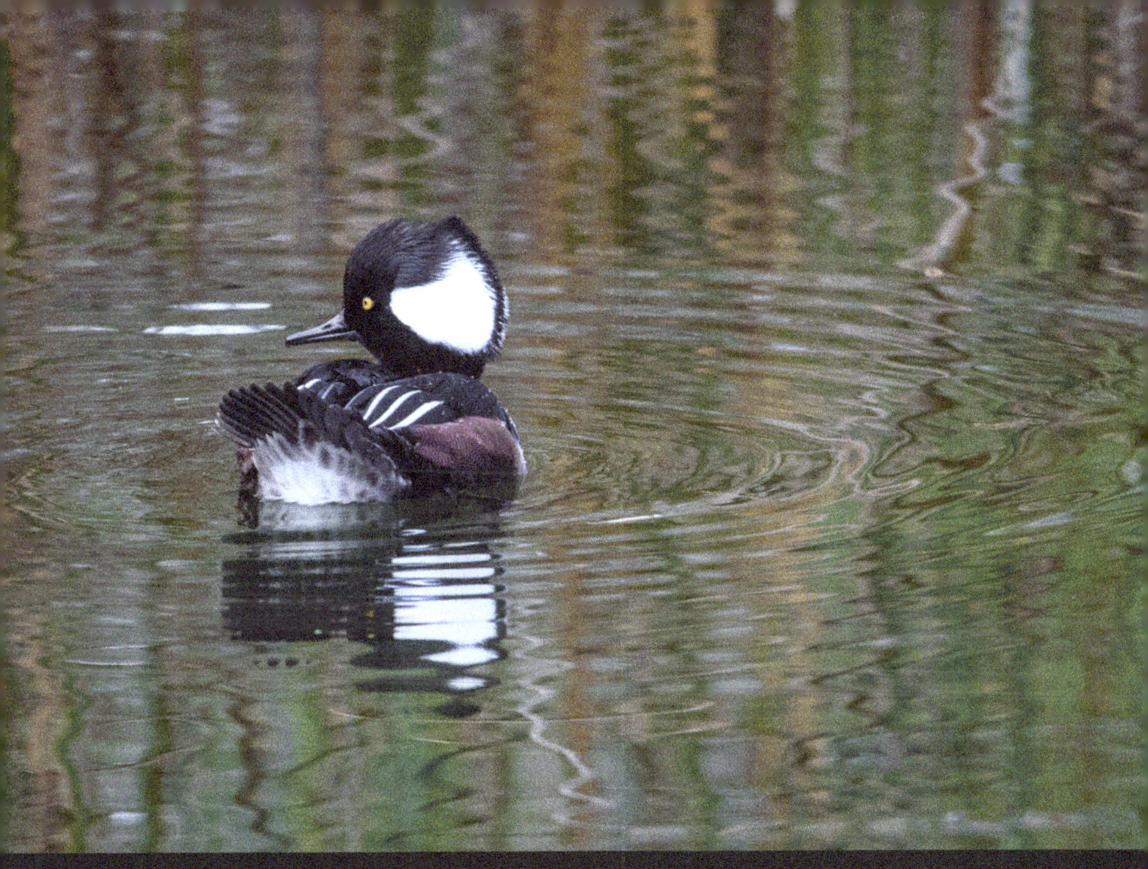

Hooded Merganser looked over his shoulder. He was showing off for an attractive female. She was ignoring him. The day was not turning out as he had hoped.

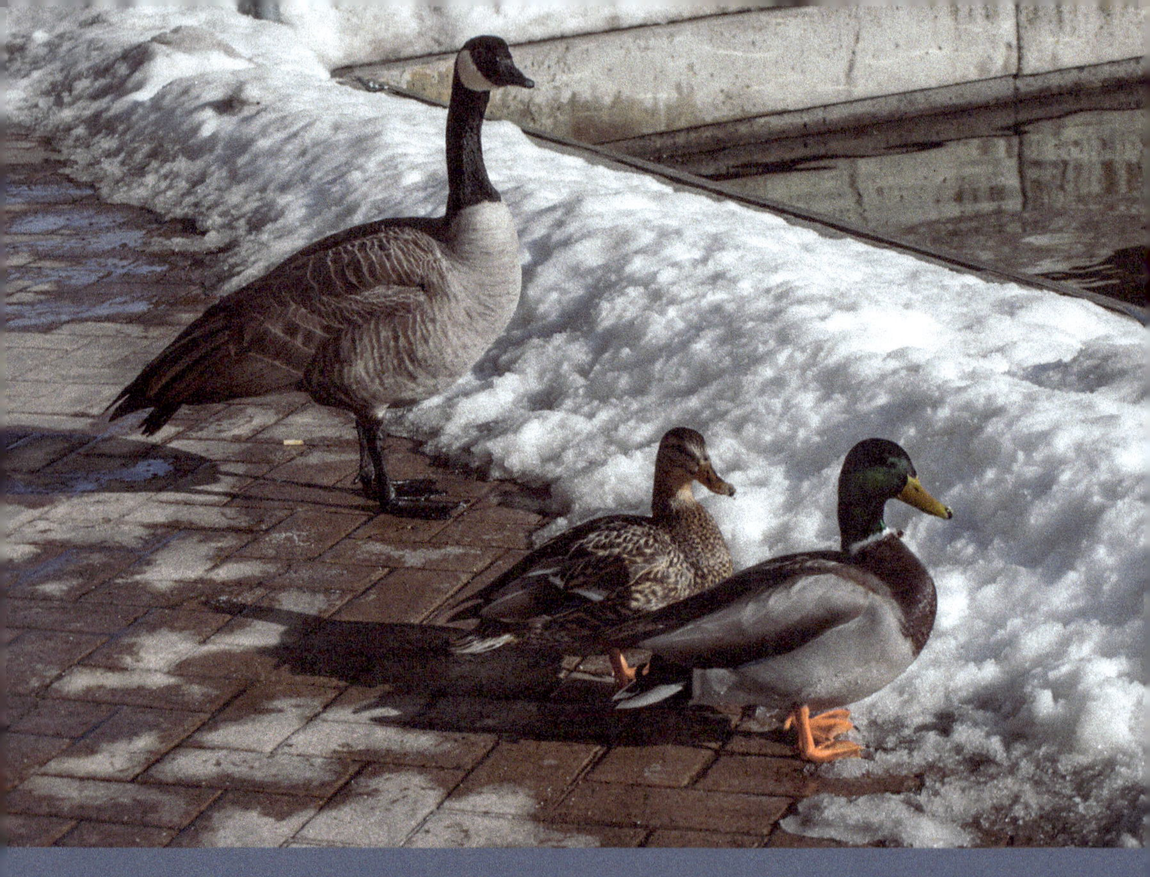

They stared at the human, wondering if he had brought food today. Goose knew he thought she was a sad loner, but she was actually a contented introvert. Flocks were too noisy for her. Ducks were quieter.

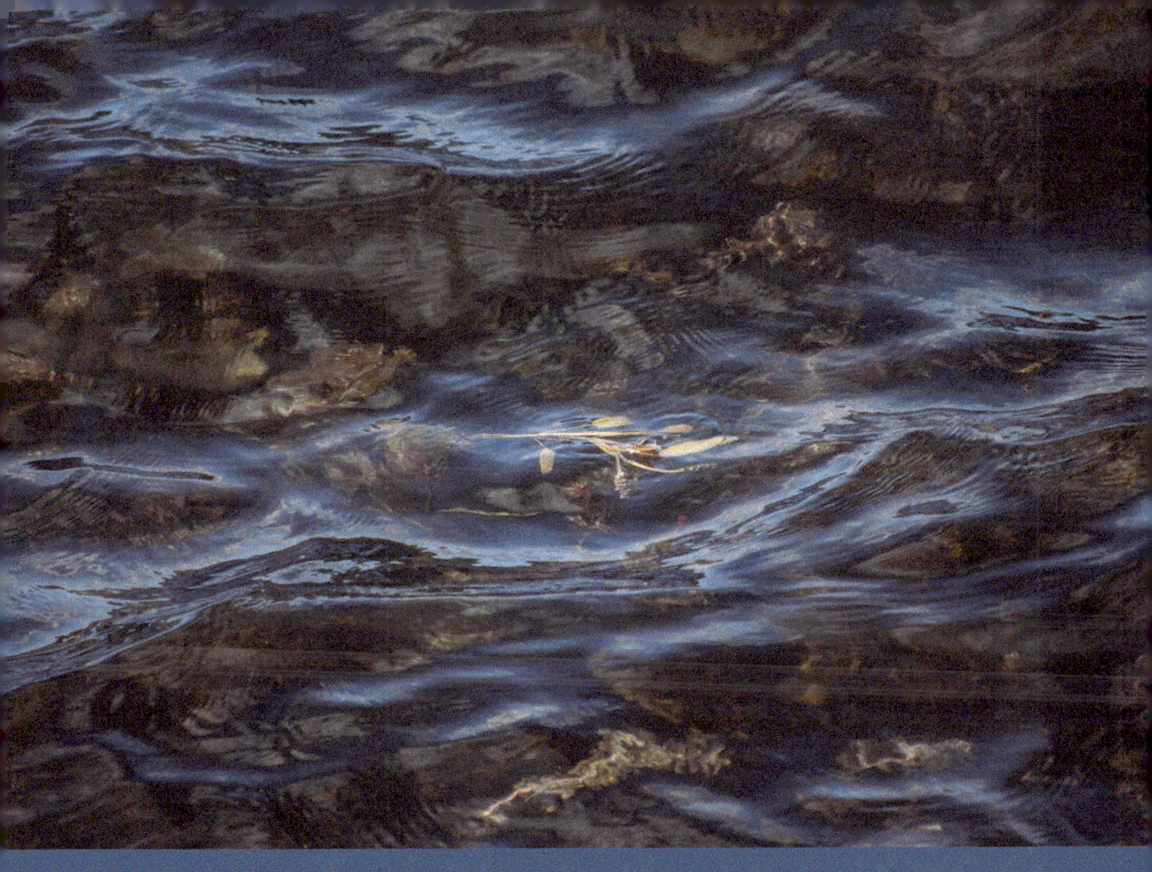

Leaves floated on the lake waters. They thanked Wind for carrying them to where they could venture into the unknown. They knew this would be their last journey.

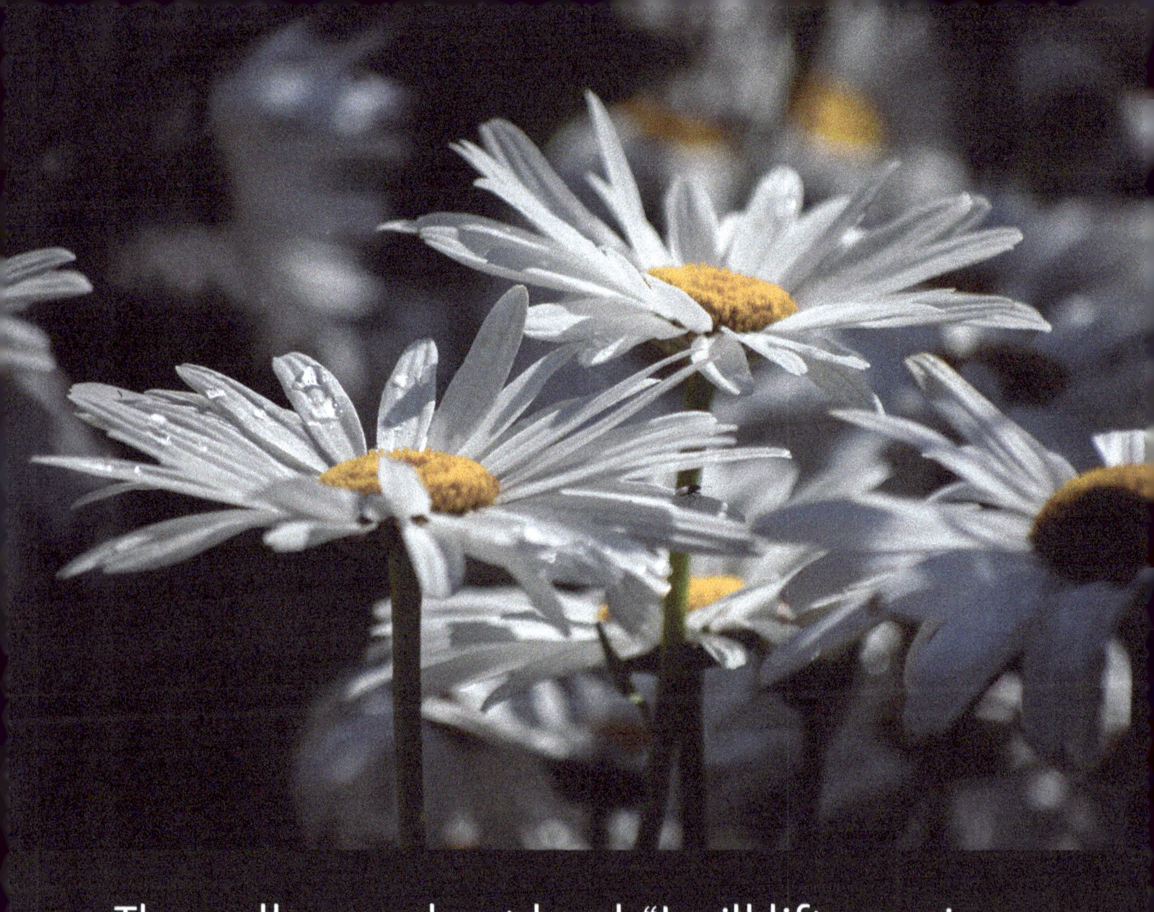

The walker read out loud, "I will lift up mine eyes unto the hills, from whence cometh my help." Daisy sighed. She was sure if the Hebrews had known her when they were writing the Psalms, they would have written, "I will lift up my petals."

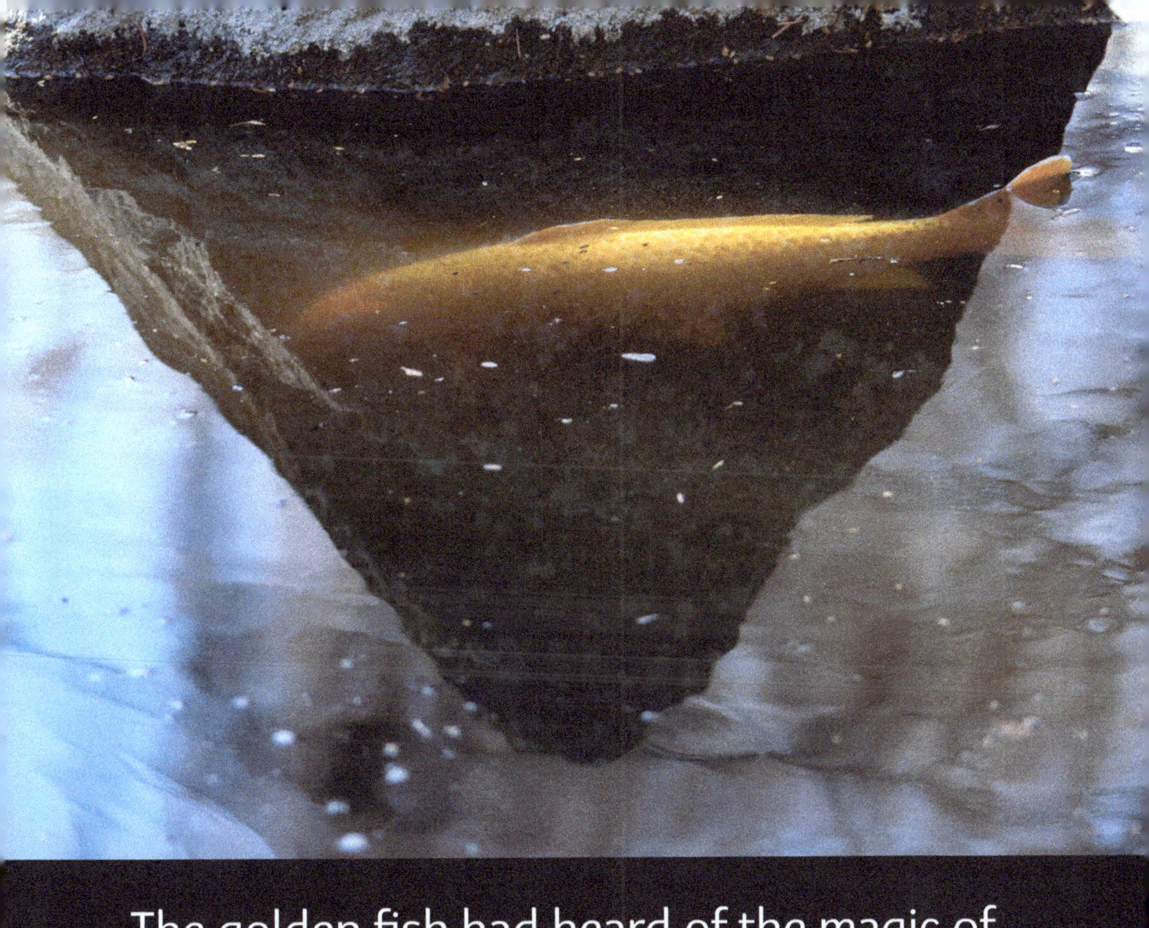

The golden fish had heard of the magic of pyramids and wondered if it work for her

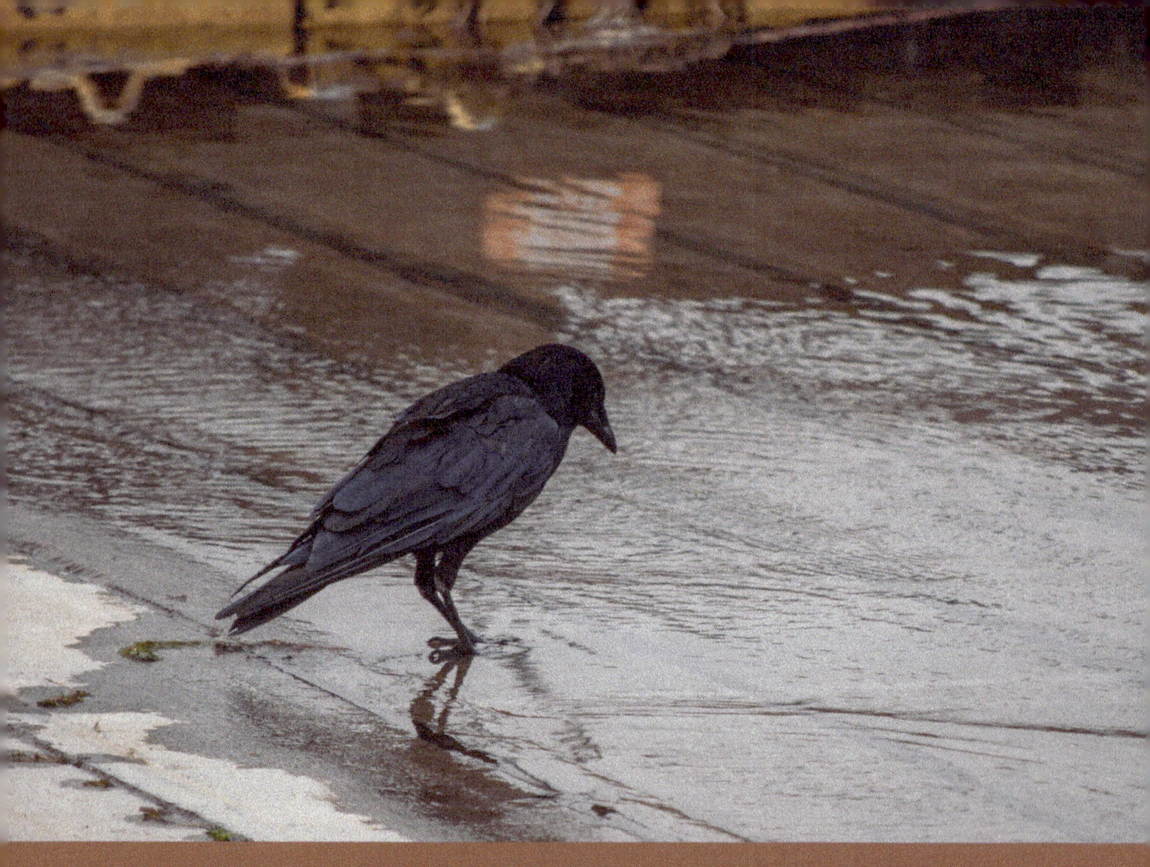

"Let's see...was it left foot forward, right foot side, wing shake...or was it right foot back, left foot back, hop, hop?" Crow was preparing for the Predator Ball and wished he had paid more attention during dancing lessons.

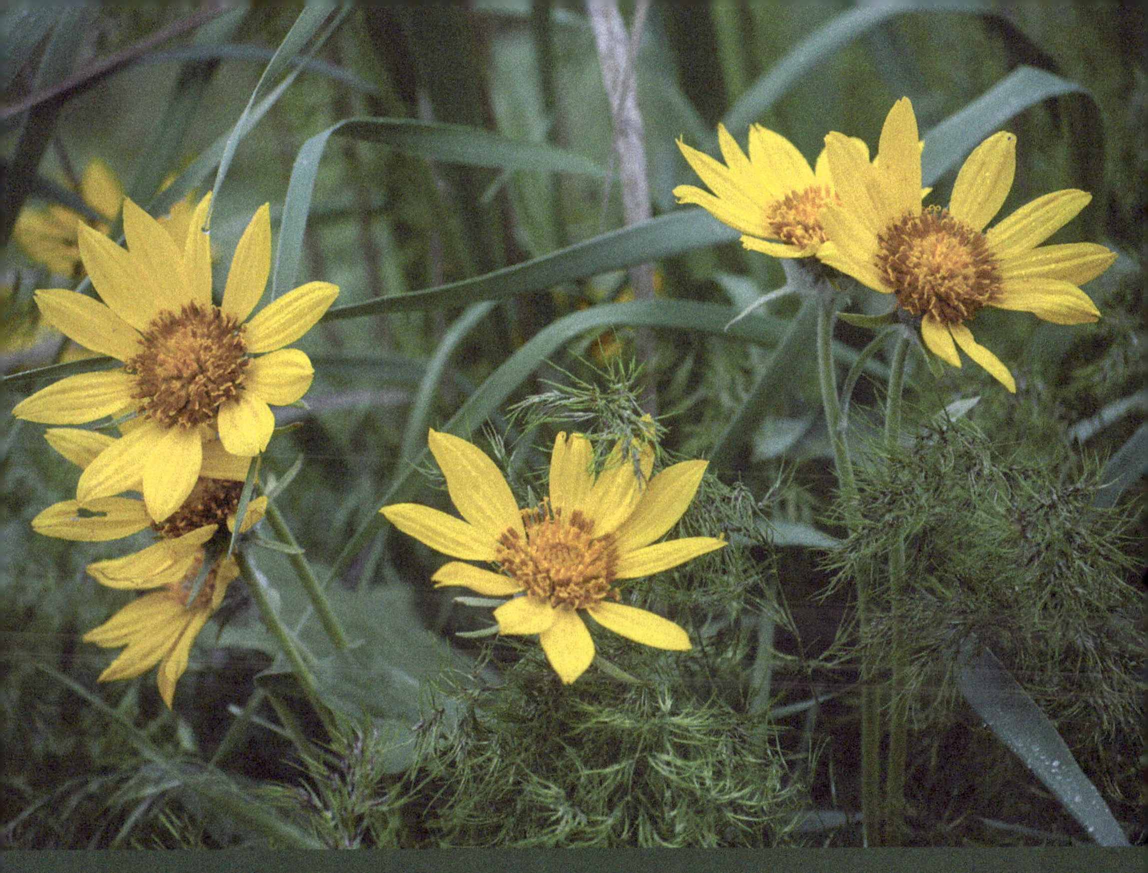

The hills were dotted with sunny flowers, beaming mightily and brightening spirits. Their lives were short so they made them count.

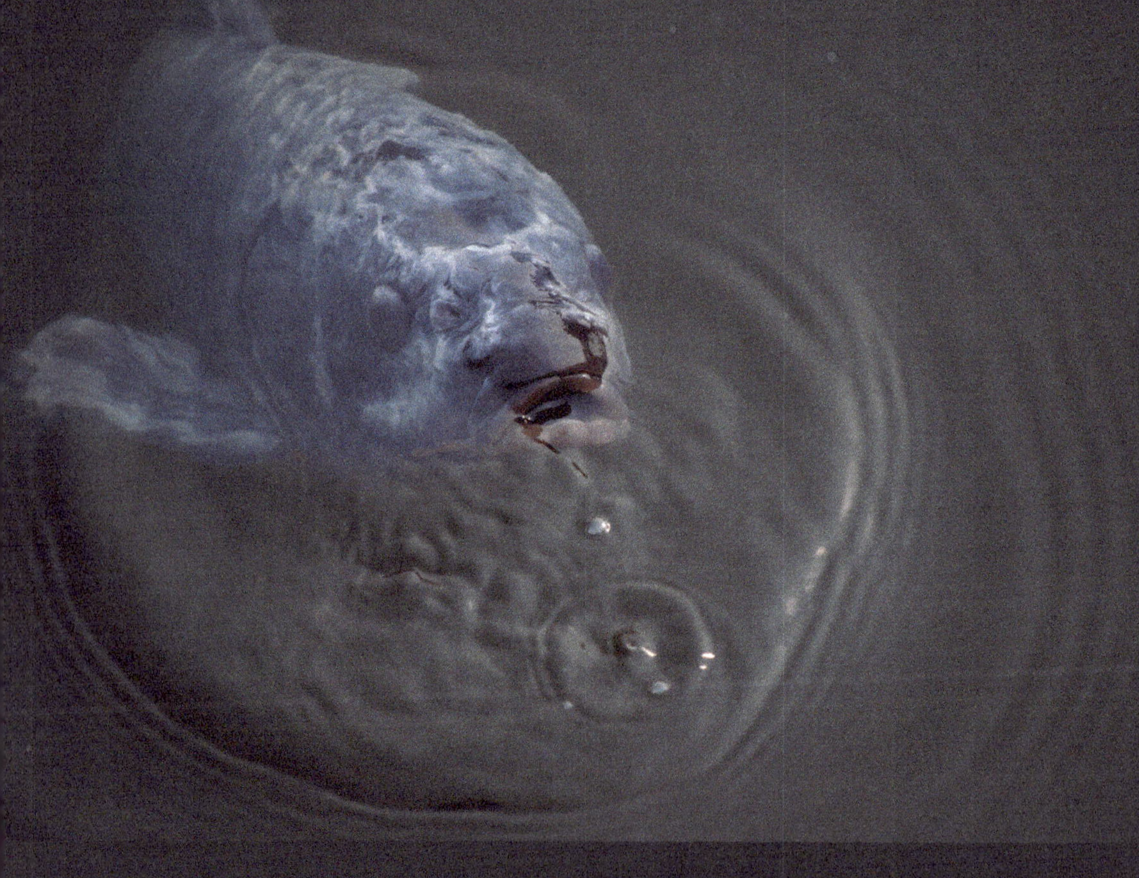

Among carp, he was considered a handsome specimen. So he was surprised to overhear humans talking about how ugly he was. It was a good lesson since he found them a most repulsive species.

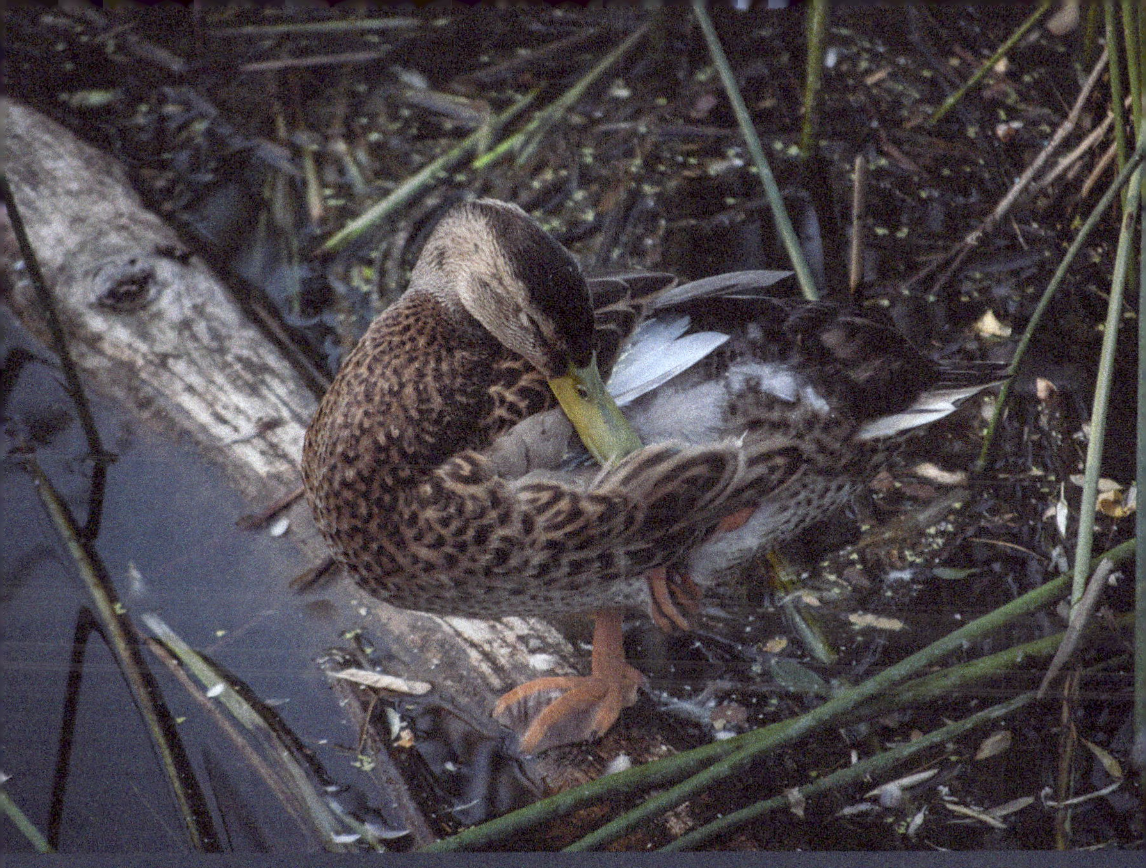

Not every duck could do a thorough preening standing on one leg. But Mallard was not just any duck. She was Queen of the Marsh. She had to set an example for her loyal subjects, even though most of them had no idea she was a queen.

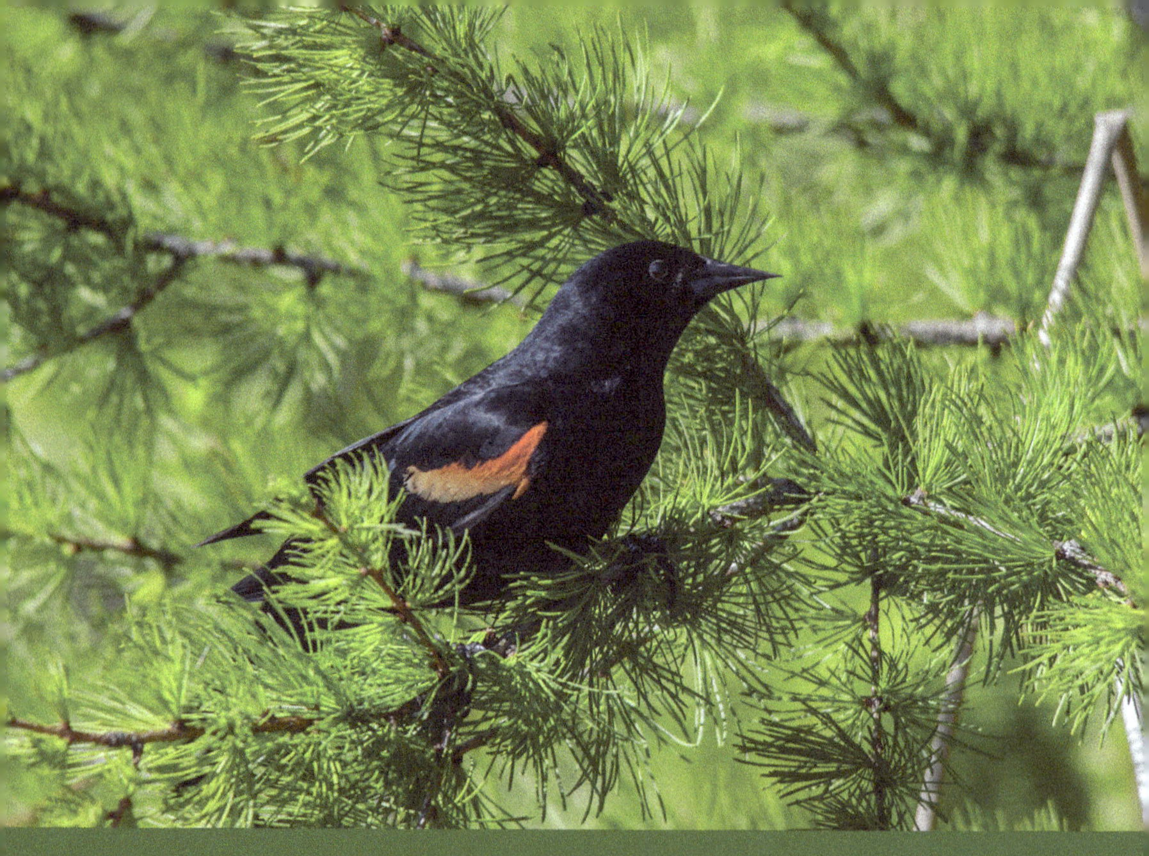

Half hidden among the tamarack needles, red-winged blackbird contemplated the hours ahead. First he would plague the osprey. Then he would chase humans away from his mate's nest. It was going to be a good day.

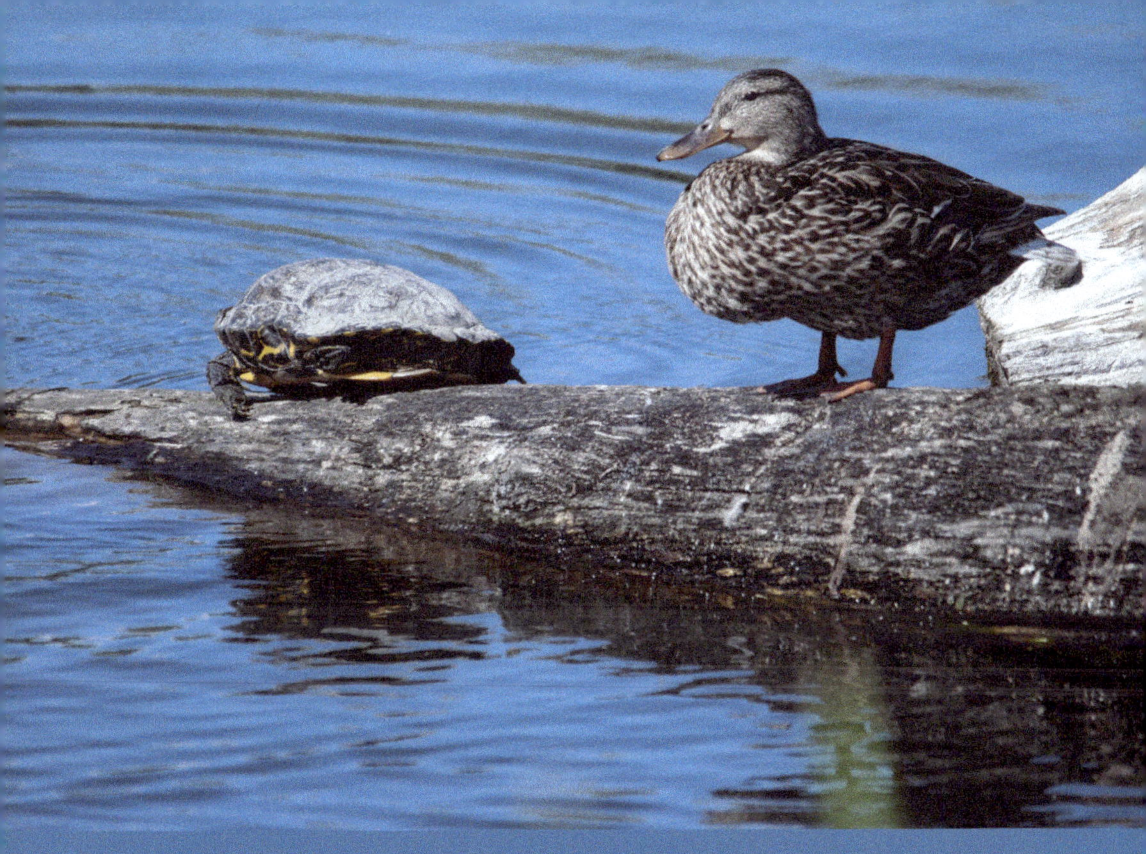

Duck could never just sit still and listen to wind and water. She was a sociable creature, convinced Turtle loved to hear her quack. Turtle listened politely until he thought he would burst out of his shell, then quietly slipped off the log.

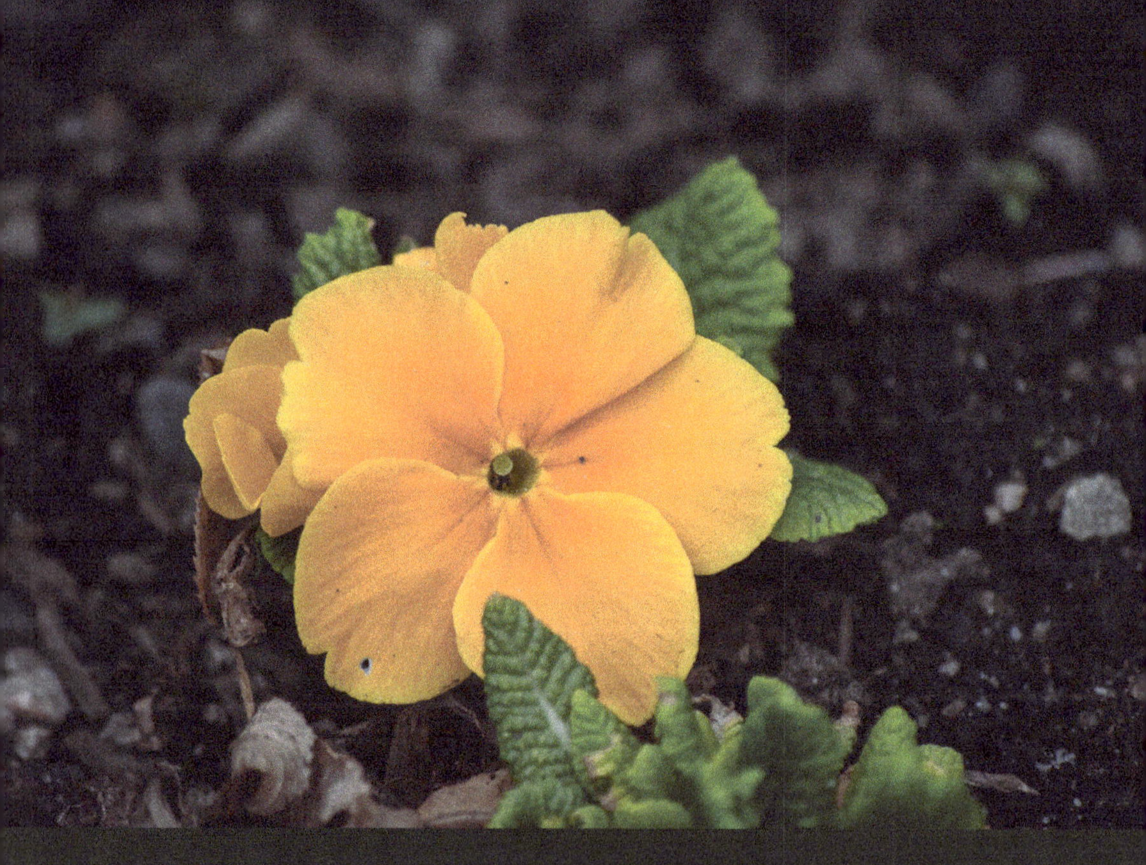

Shy Primrose tried desperately to hide behind her neighbor, but nothing could disguise the splendor of her bright dress.

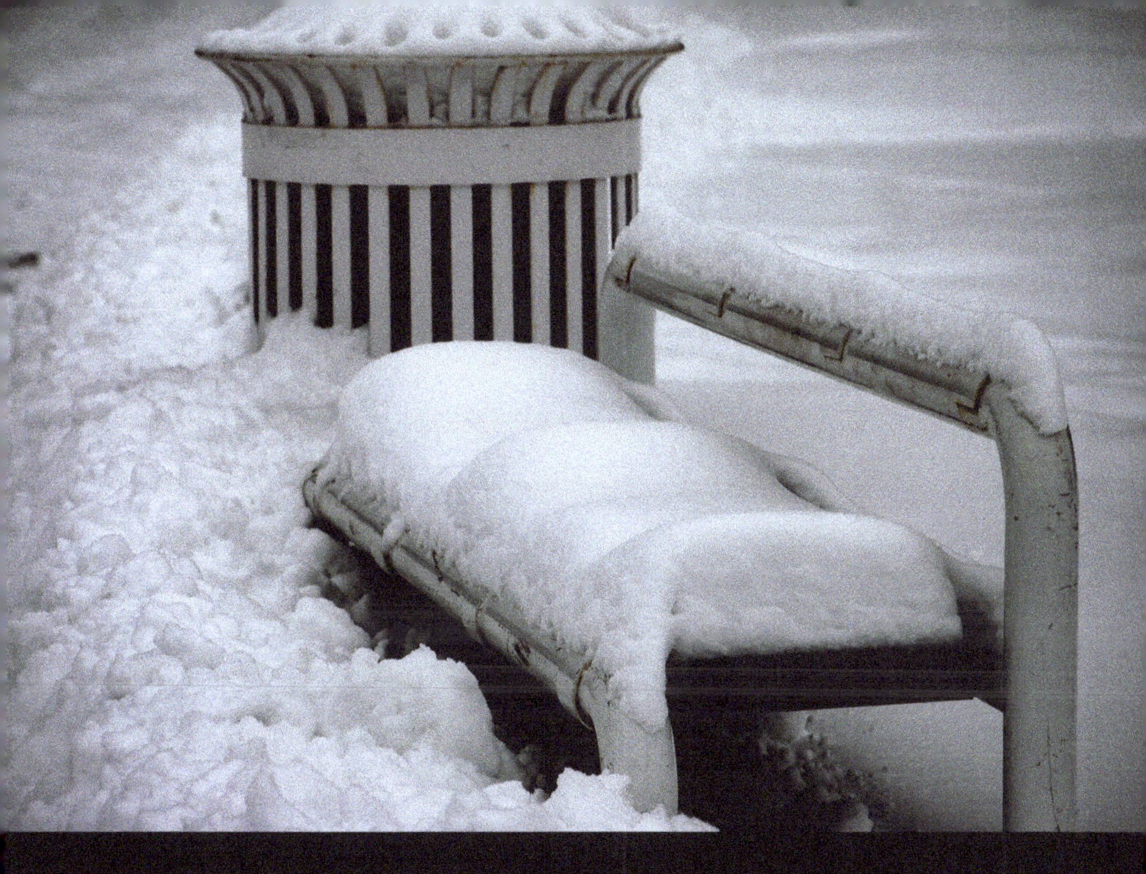

Garbage Can could see Bench was getting all sentimental about the warm bums of summer. "Cheer up, Pal. Remember the farters."

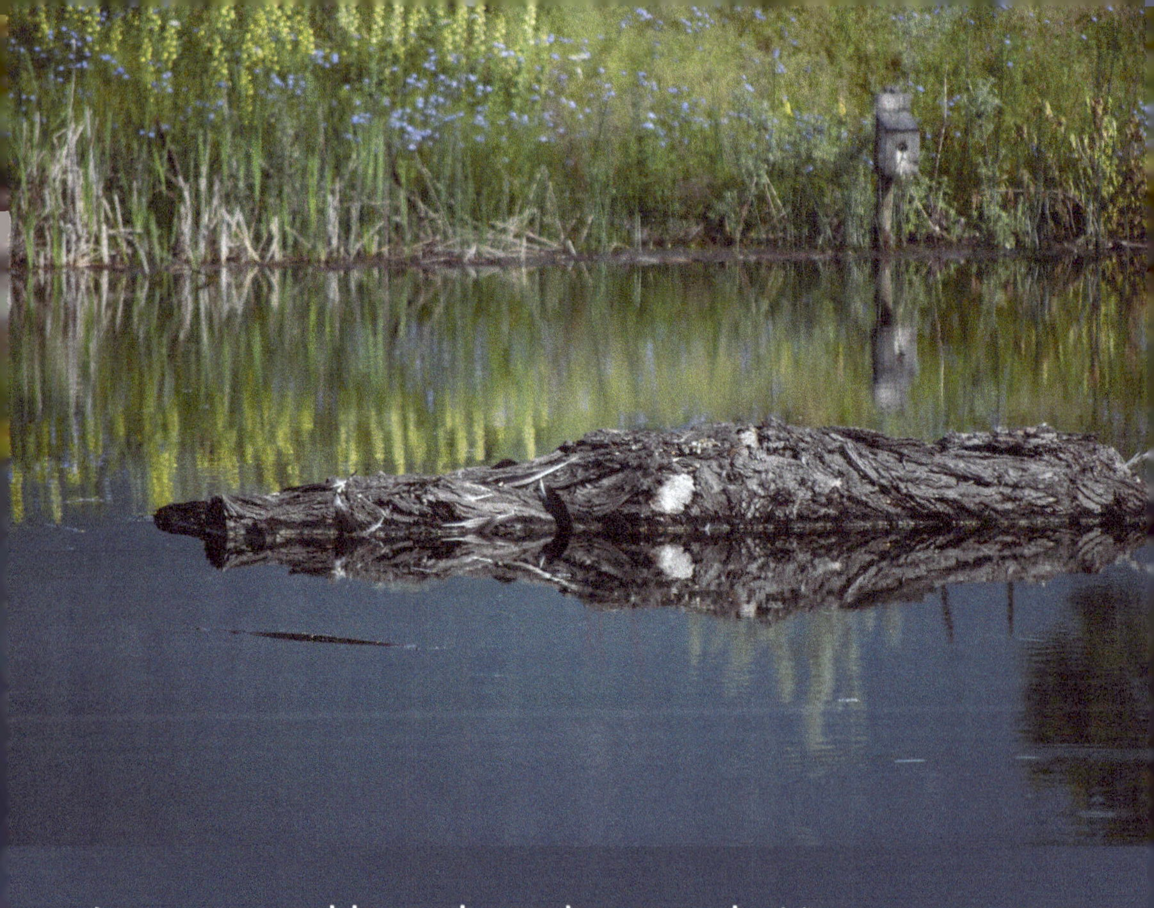

Log enjoyed his job in the marsh. He met many mallards and coots and even a Great Blue Heron. Still, when rising waters lifted him from his resting place, he found himself yearning for adventure in the lake beyond.

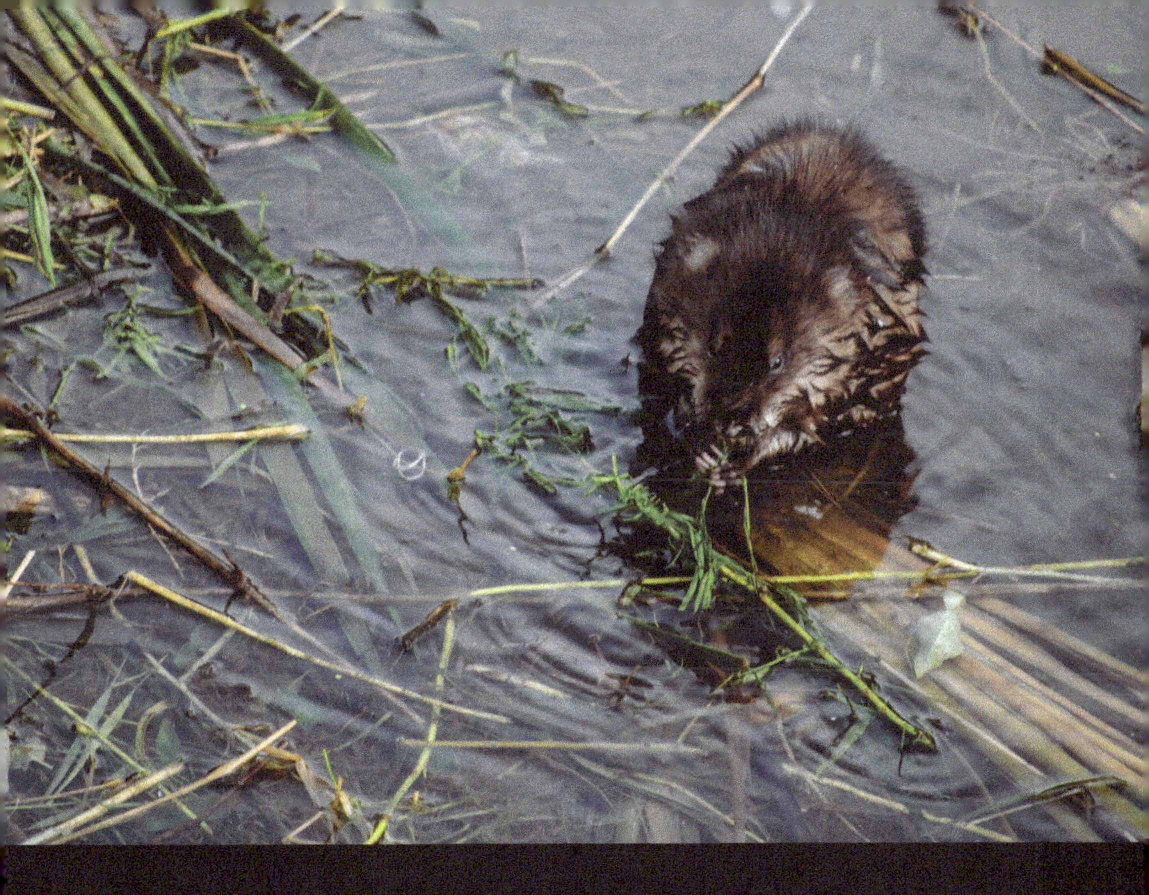

Muskrat was proud of her soft fur. When anyone asked how she kept it so shiny, she always said, "I eat plants. And I wash every day." She hated the folksong about smelly muskrats, which showed how little humans knew about seductive aromas

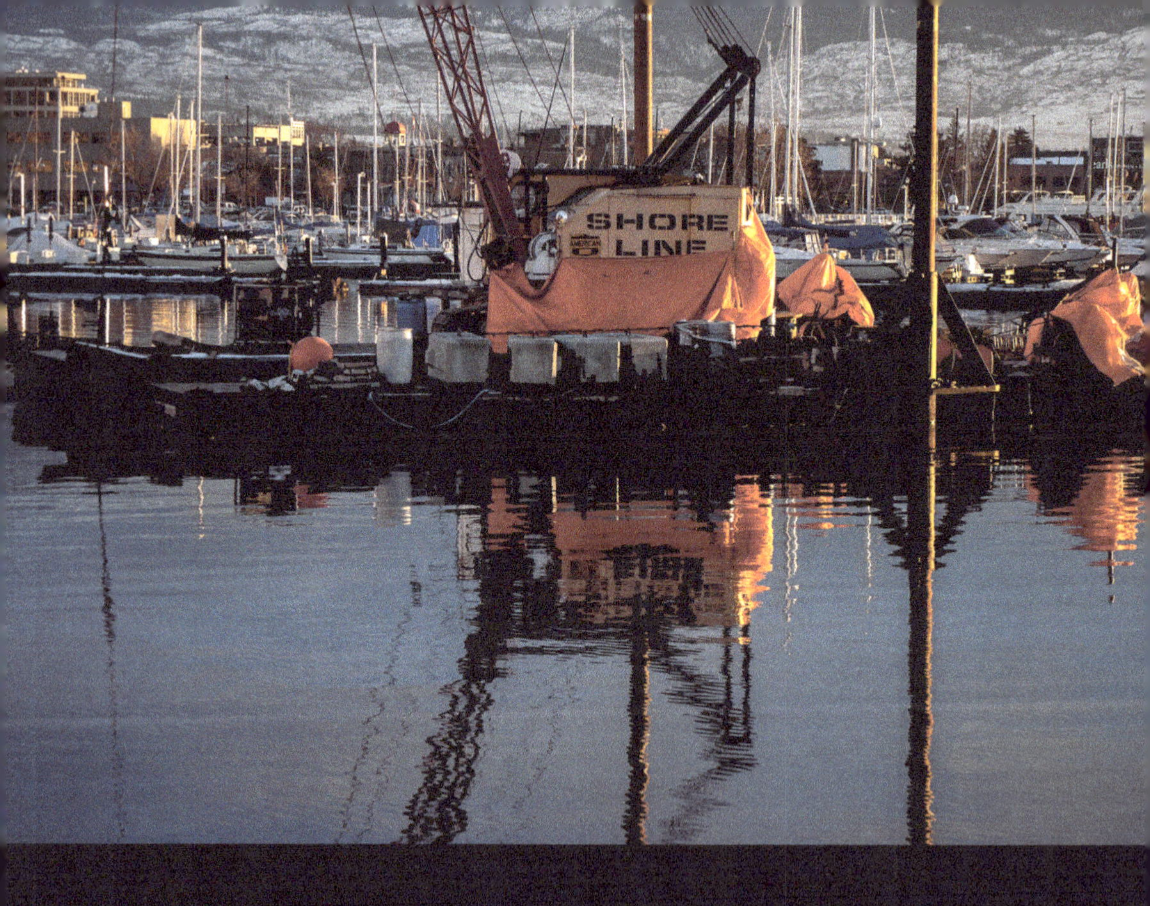

Crane hooted with delight. He hung around the waterfront for months. No one looked at him until Sun lit up the tarps. Then he was the darling of the day. Silly humans snapped dozens of photographs they would never look at

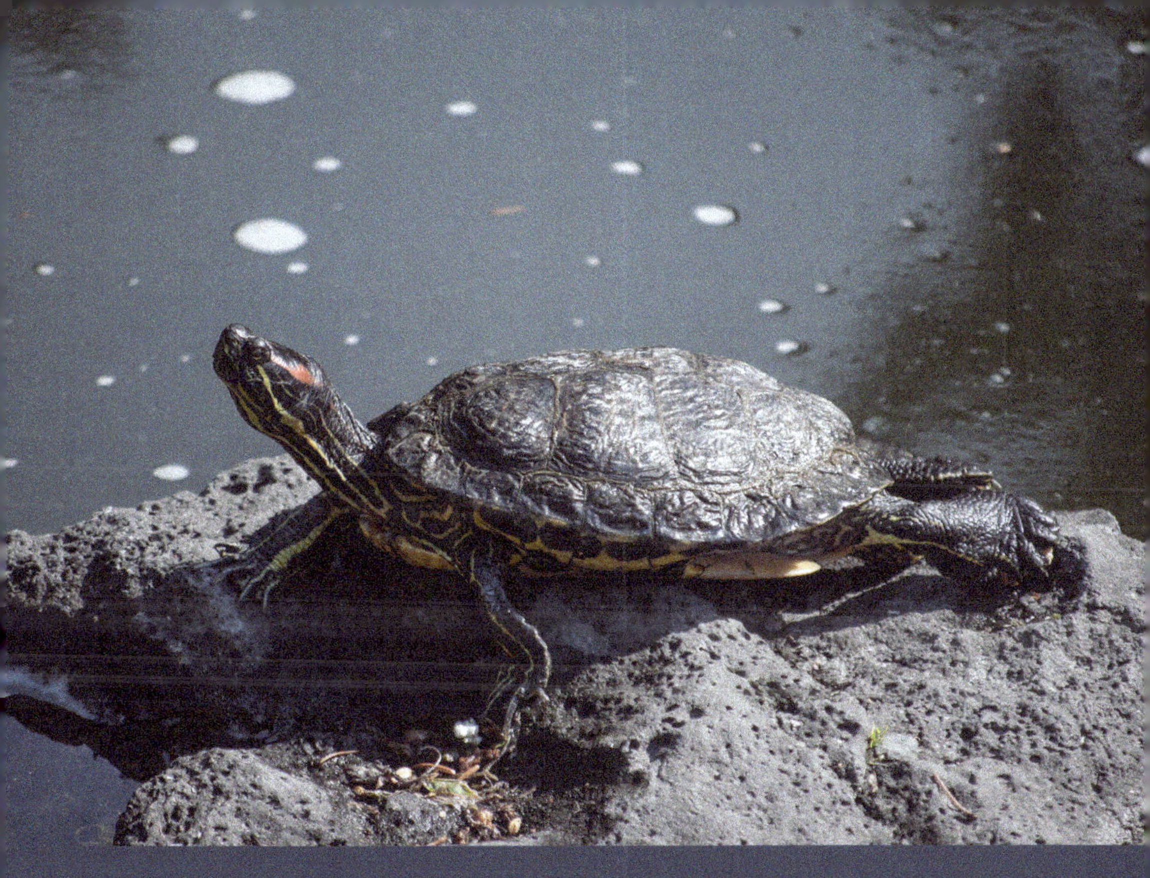

Before Mud Time, Turtle had company on his rock. As Warm Time neared, he looked forward to seeing the young turtles again. So far, none of them had returned, and he was becoming resigned to spending Warm Time alone.

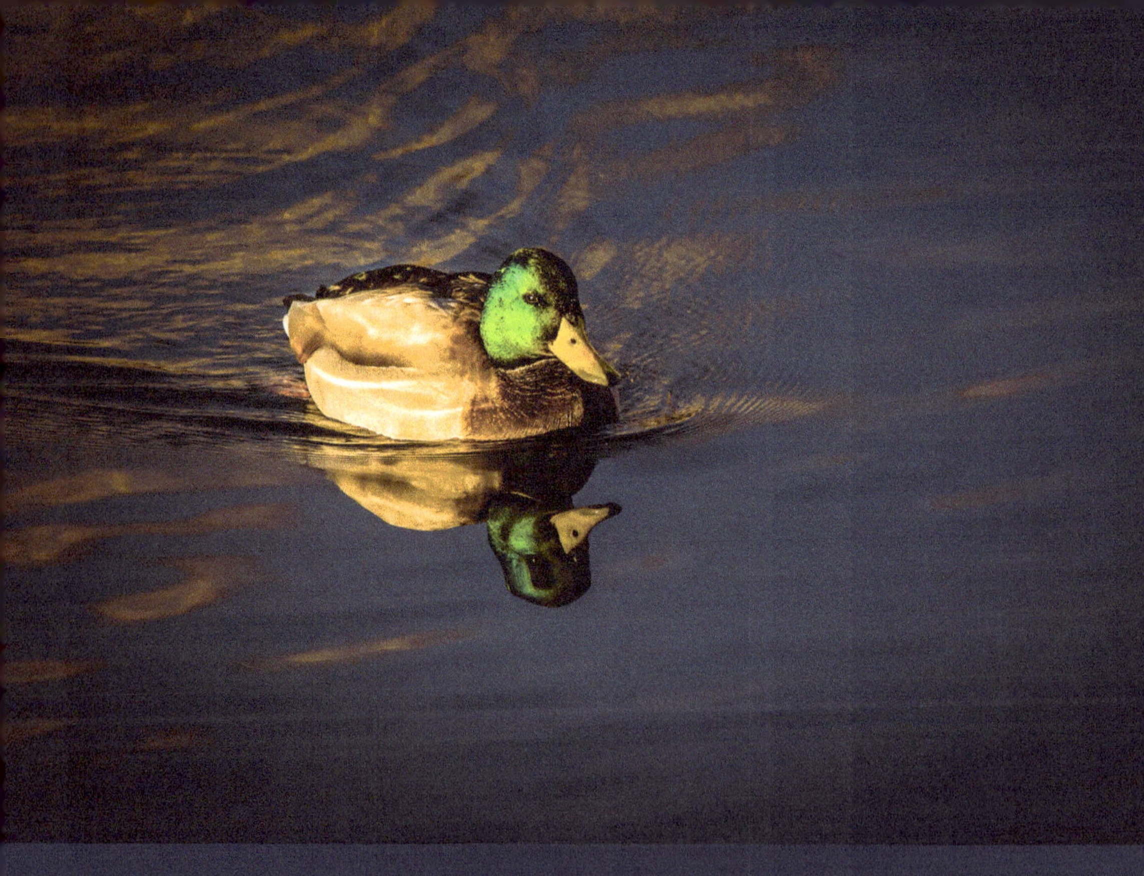

Mallard wondered why humans kept bringing odd things to their eyes and pointing at him. He knew nothing about smart phones and cameras, nor about the play of sun on his feathers. He did know humans had strange habits.

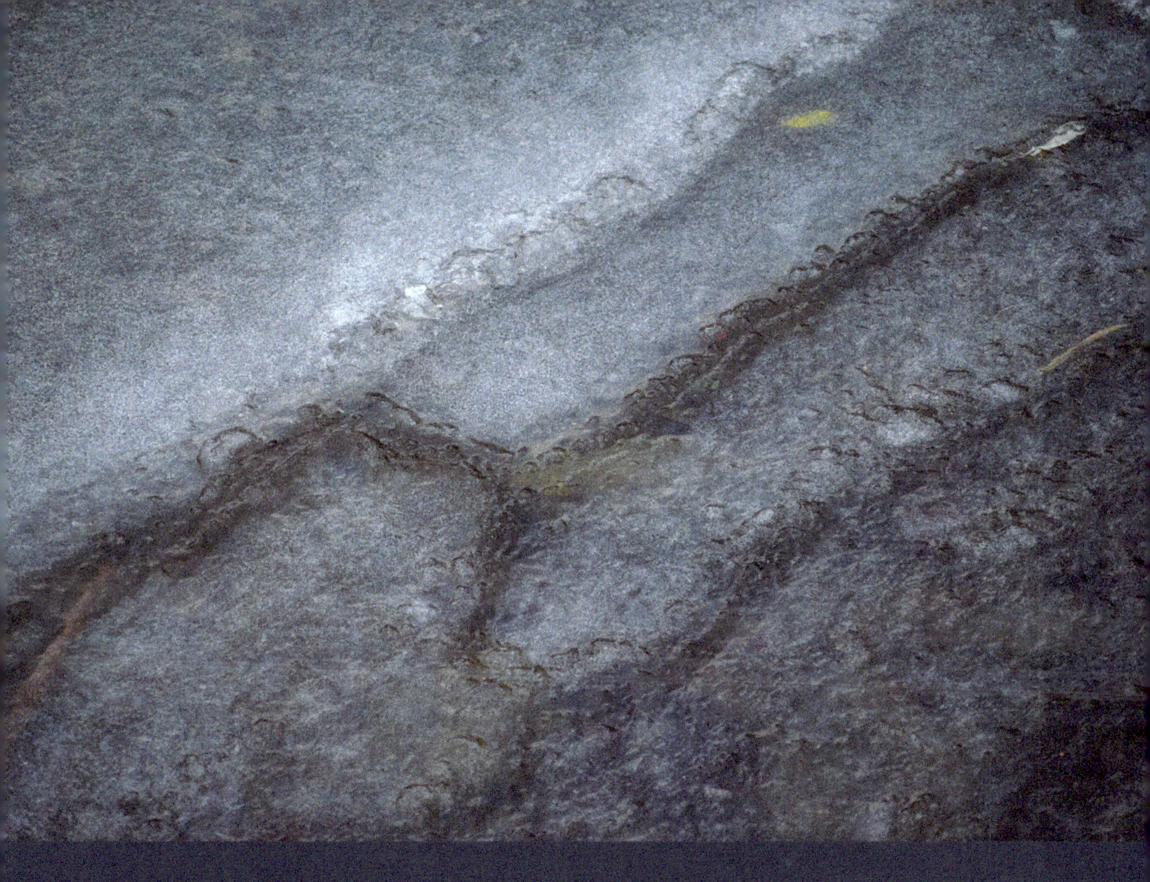

Water waited all year for cold weather to return. He loved to play Snakes and Ladders. He did not know the game's rules, but it did not matter. He made up his own.

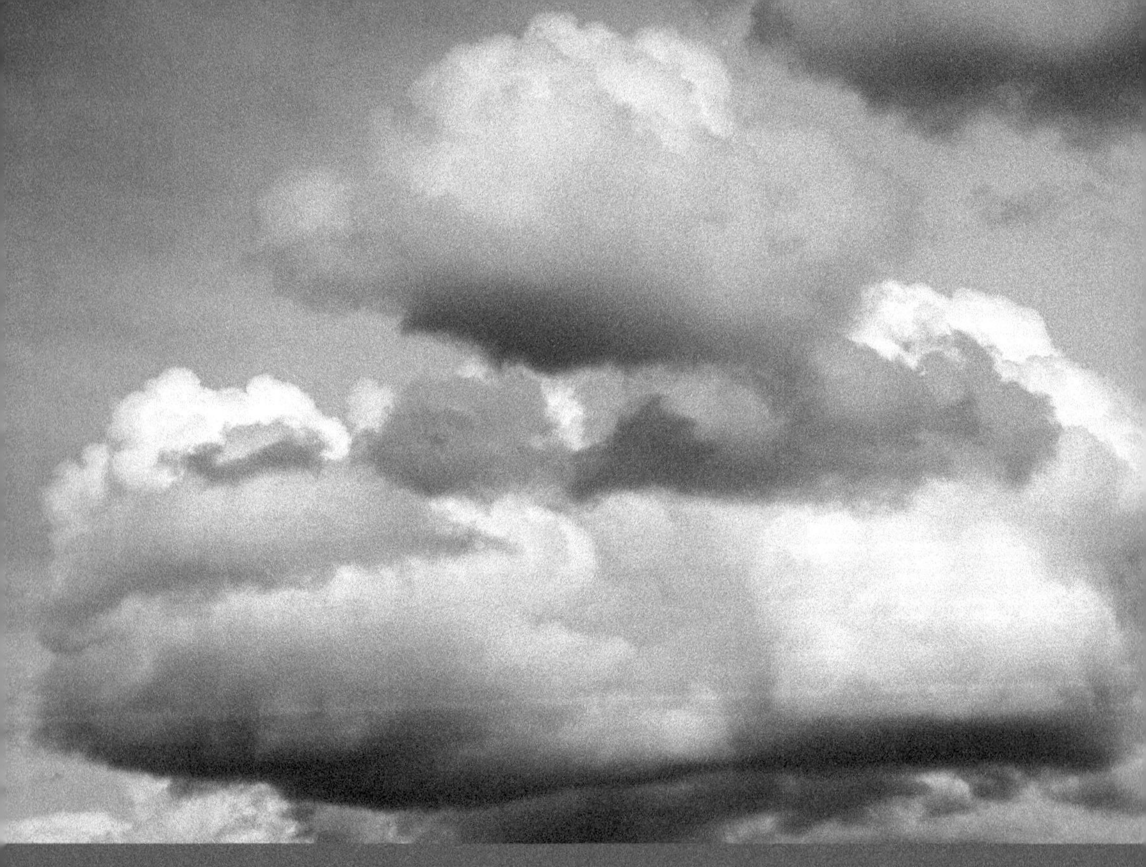

Mitzi stuck her neck out. "Waldo, I have something to tell you." Before he had time to worry, Baby King Kong popped up between them. They all laughed so hard they rained.

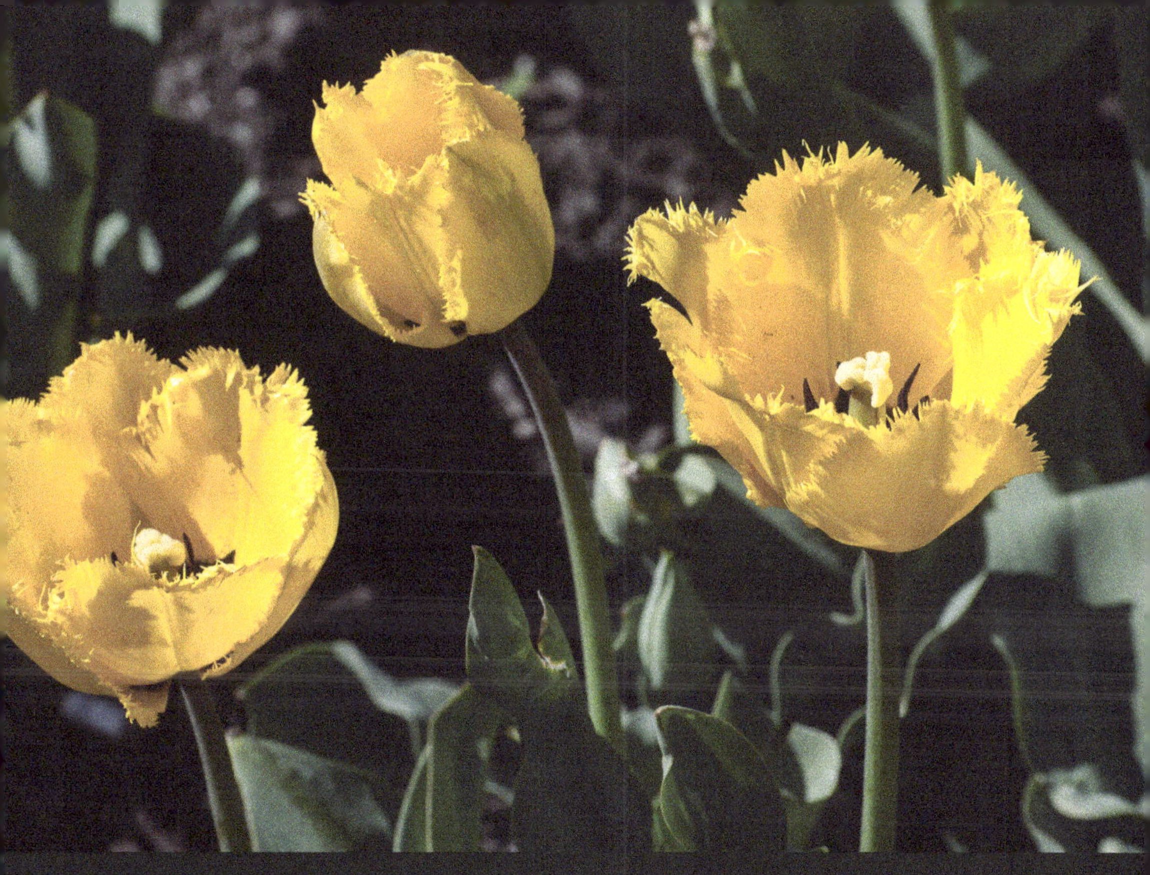

They were eager to become a trio, but one of them was developing slowly. They feared they would lose their edge before he grew enough to harmonize with them.

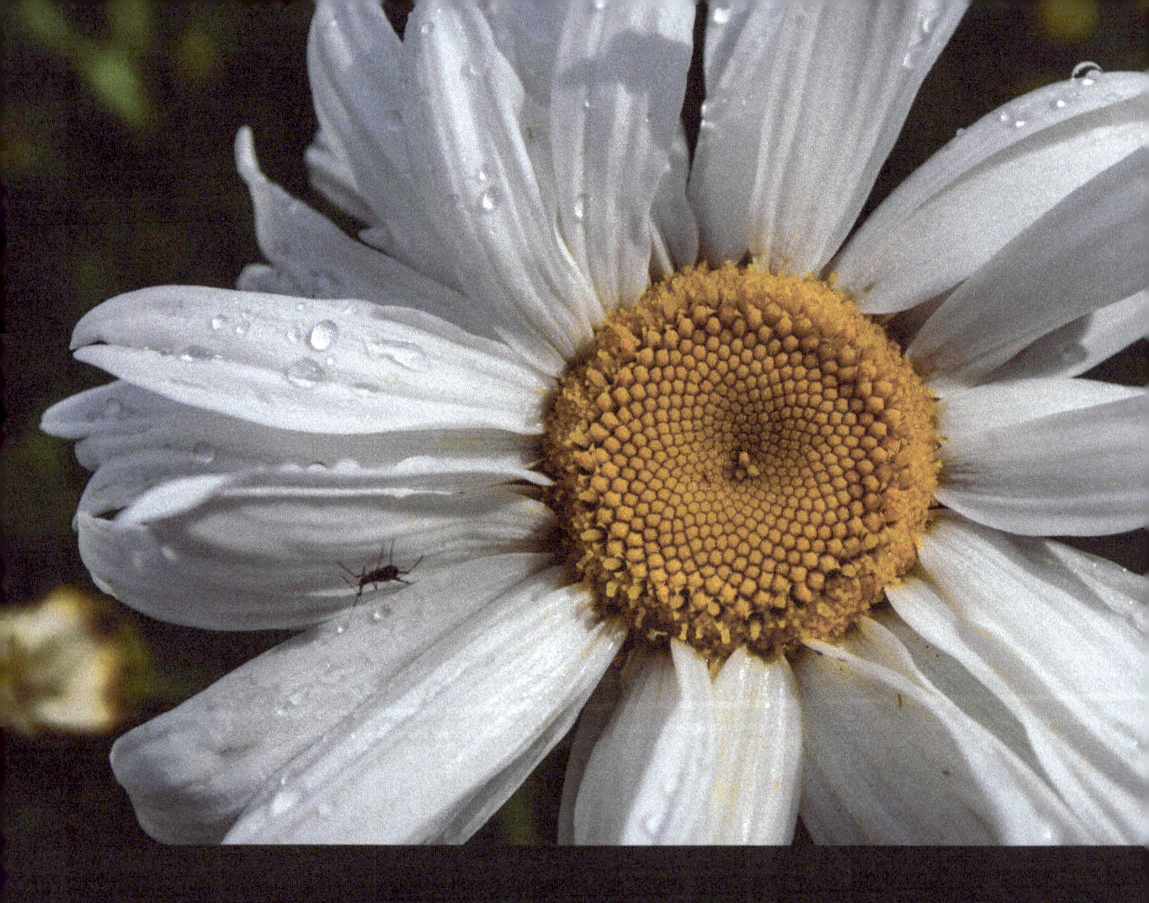

"Stop tickling me!" Daisy sighed. Bug did not understand her language, but it did not matter. No protest would have stopped him. He had a family to feed, and Daisy offered tasty tidbits

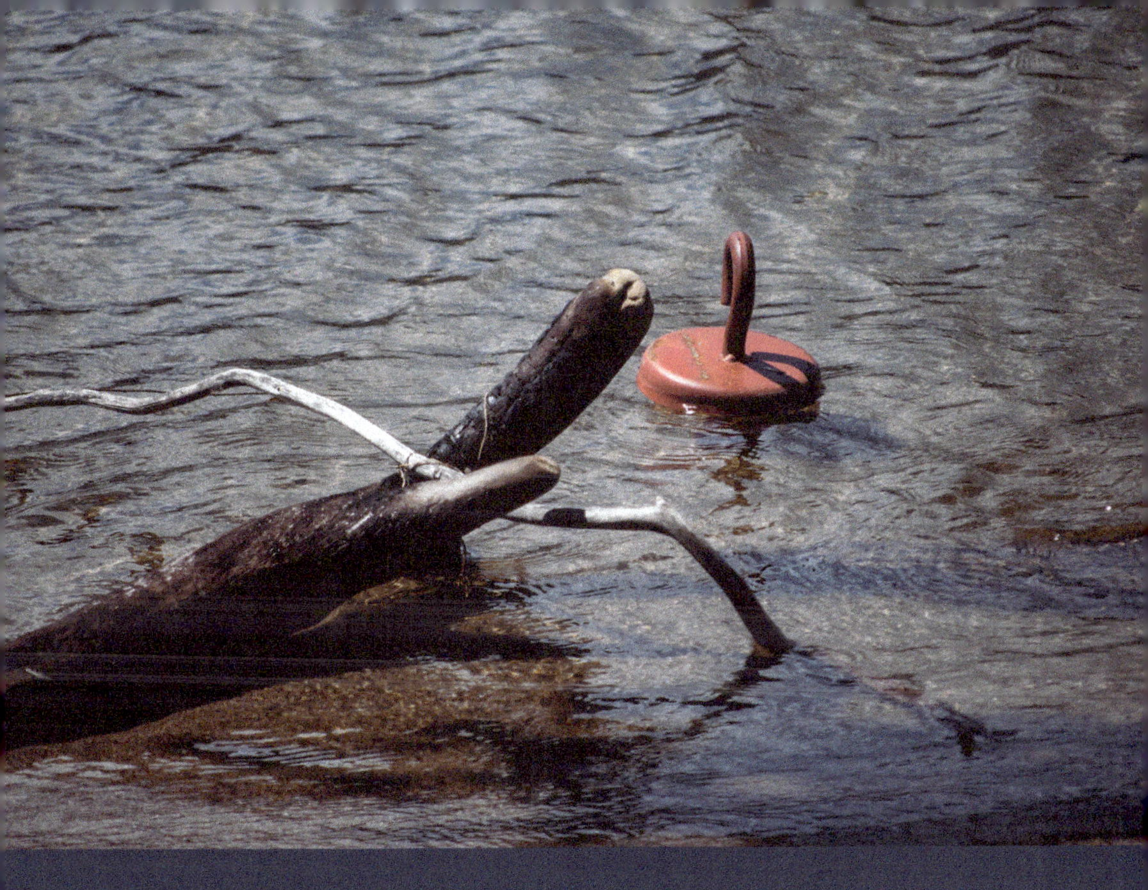

"I was holding down bladder dam, protecting the city from floods, when all the water whooshed out of her." Branch and Limb sighed. Hook had no idea they had been through drought and fire and flood. A mere "whoosh" seemed so mundane.

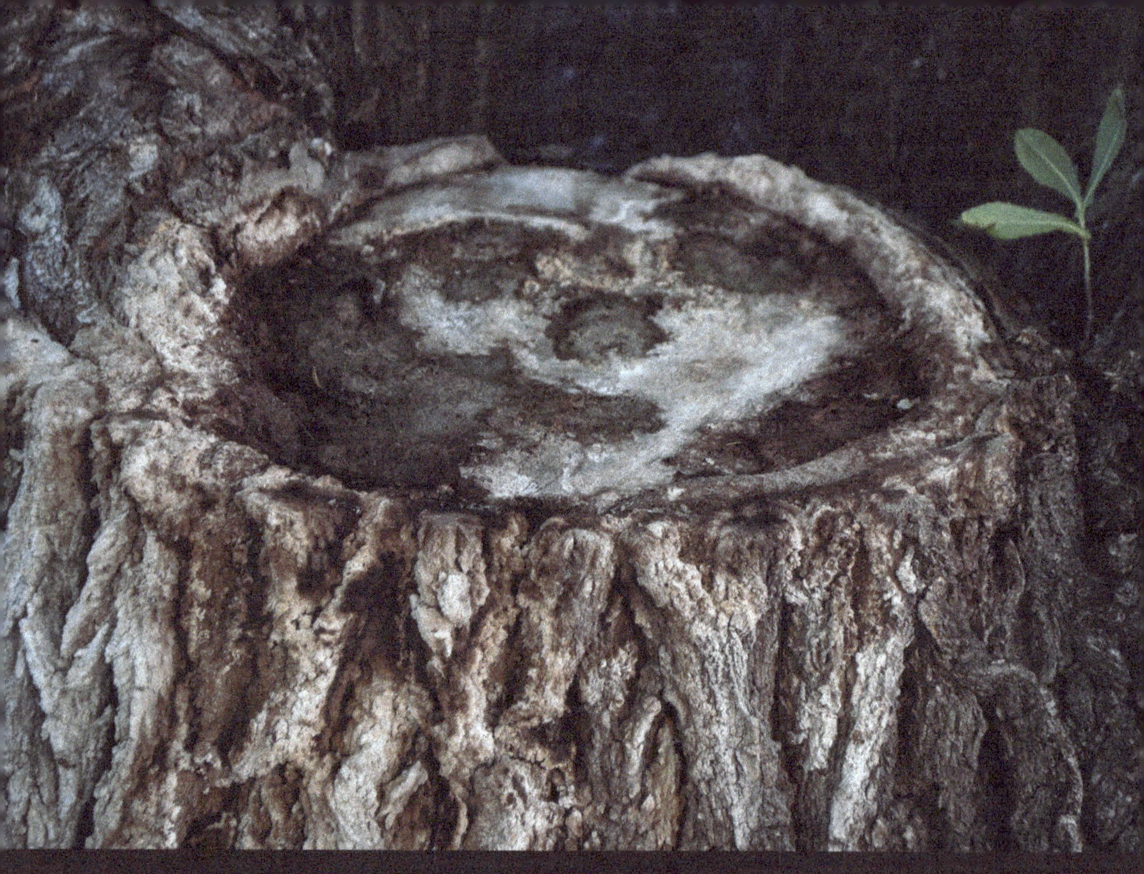

"I'll name you Abelardo," said the child who discovered the face on a stump. "It means kind, and you very kindly gave me a good place to sit and dream."

ABOUT THE AUTHOR

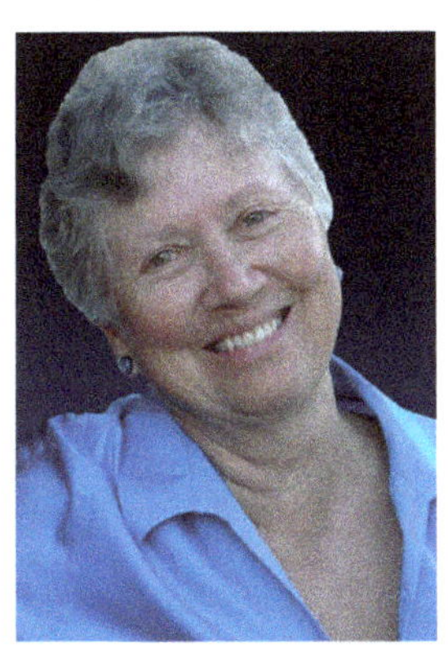

Cathryn Wellner is a writer, photographer and storyteller living in Kelowna, British Columbia, Canada. Her recent books include:

Small Scale Stories series (*That Tree Talked to Me, Parts of Me Are Still Amazing, The Disappearing Pumpkin Choir, In the Shelter of Each Other, Your Task Is to Be Admired, In the Country of Plastic*)

Essay collections (*Hope Wins & Feisty Aging*)

In the Hug of Hills

Millie's Foster Family children's series (*Millie's Feathered Foster Family, Turkey Baby and the Hungry Hawk, Turkey Baby Finds Her Magic*)

You can find links to these and her other books at cathrynwellner.com. Contact her at cathryn@cathrynwellner.com or 778-478-2760. Her photographs can be found on her Web site, as well as on Facebook and Instagram.

BE A BOOK REVIEW ANGEL

If you enjoyed this book, please post a review on Amazon or Goodreads. Share it with friends and rave about it on social media. You can contact the author at cathryn@cathrynwellner.com.

Authors rely on their readers to help spread the word about books they like. People who review books are special kinds of reader angels. I guarantee when you review this book, or any other book that has given you pleasure in any way, you'll feel those wings poking out your back. Look closely in the mirror, and you might even see a halo.

Credits

Fonts used on cover and some interior pages: Saltash, Sun Kissed, and Northwell. Font used in stories: Bw Surco. Logo font: Ed's Market. Face on dedication page by Rebecca McMeen. All fonts and graphic elements are licensed through DesignCuts.

Text and photographs by Cathryn Wellner. The book was designed in Photoshop.

Thank you to the creative people who designed the unique fonts and elements incorporated in this book. I continually learn from you.

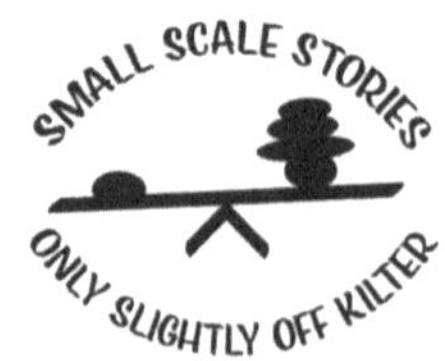

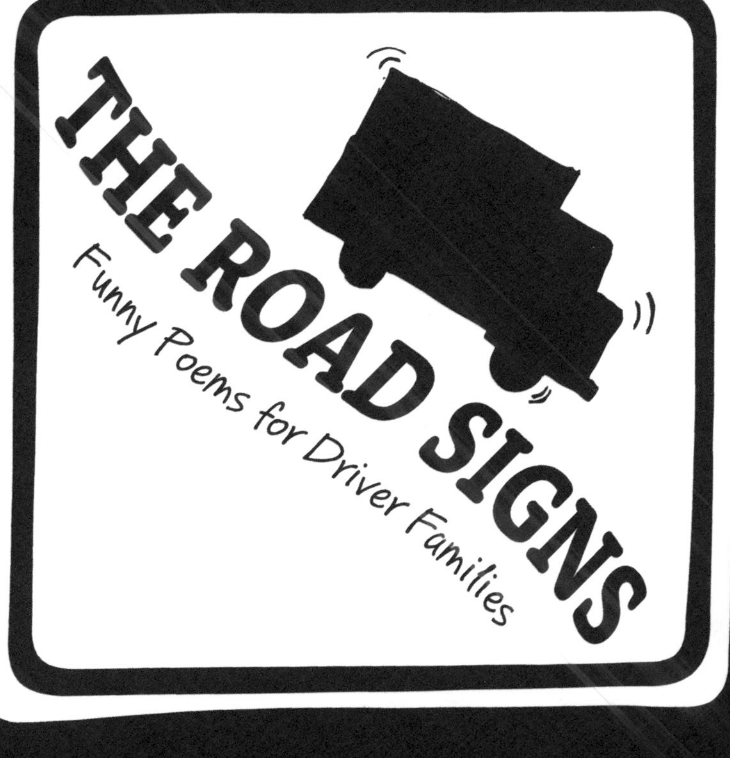

THE ROAD SIGNS
Funny Poems for Driver Families

THE ROAD SIGNS

First Edition: April 2026
Text Copyright © 2026 by Juan Manuel Hernandez Gonzalez (Meño)
Art Copyright © 2026 by Ordinal LLC

Published by:
Ordinal LLC
USA, www.ordinalbooks.com

Cover, Illustrations, and Design by: Meño

www.ordinalbooks.com
Copyright © Ordinal LLC

ISBN: 978-1-972050-00-2

To the Driver Families

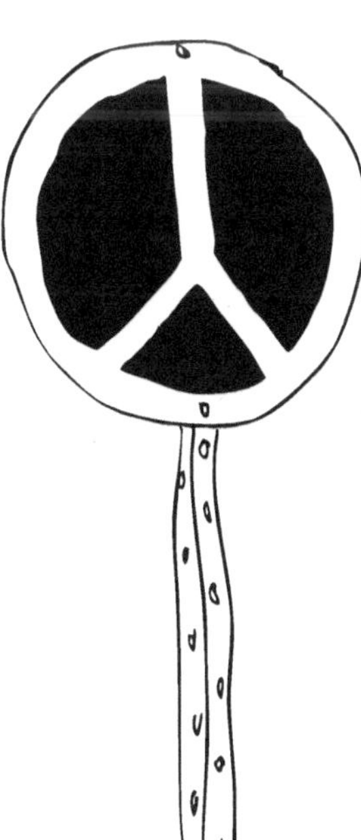

Begin a work

Begin a work...
what a difficult task.

Keep working on it...
what a difficult task.

But if you
keep
and keep
and keep
and keep
and keep
and...

Note 1: This poem continues on page 56 of this book, but don't skip to it until you've read the rest of the pages before.

Note 2: But if you are anxiouss to read it—**skip to it right now!**

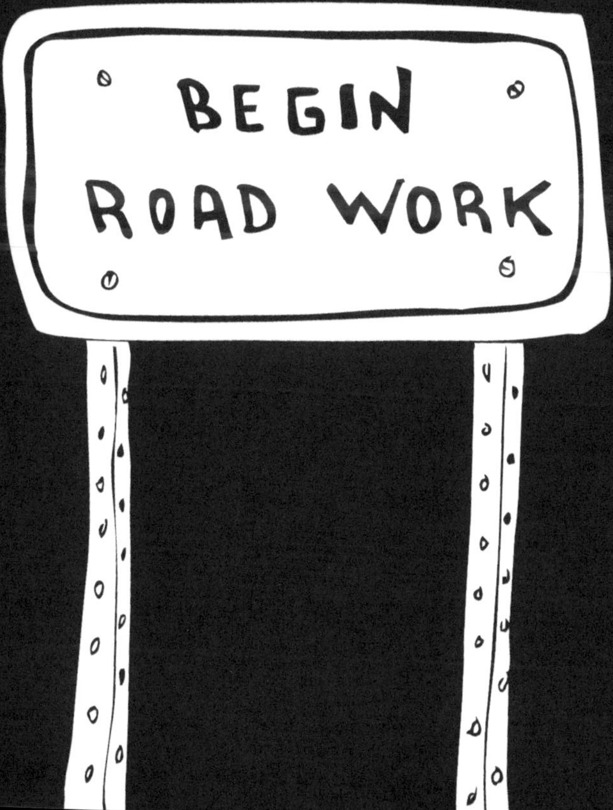

BEGIN
ROAD WORK

Dear deer

Dear Deer,
please, don't you dare
to cross the line.

Don't even think about it!

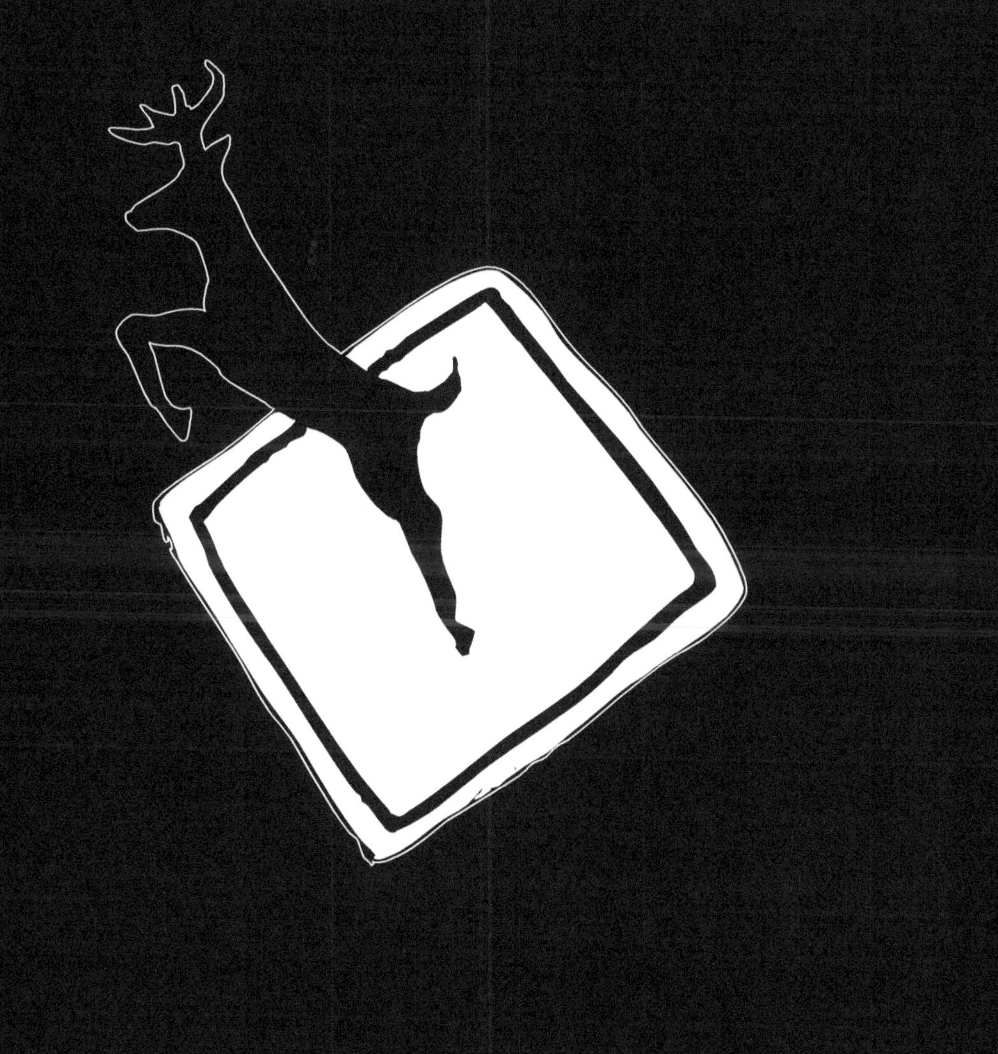

Flat tire

What a nightmare!
Have you ever heard the scream
of a flat tire?
It is horrible;
it scares me to death.

If you hear it,
don't panic or slam your brakes!
Just slow down...
and down...
and down...
until you don't hear anything else.

And then—and only then—
you can scream like a crazy man for help!

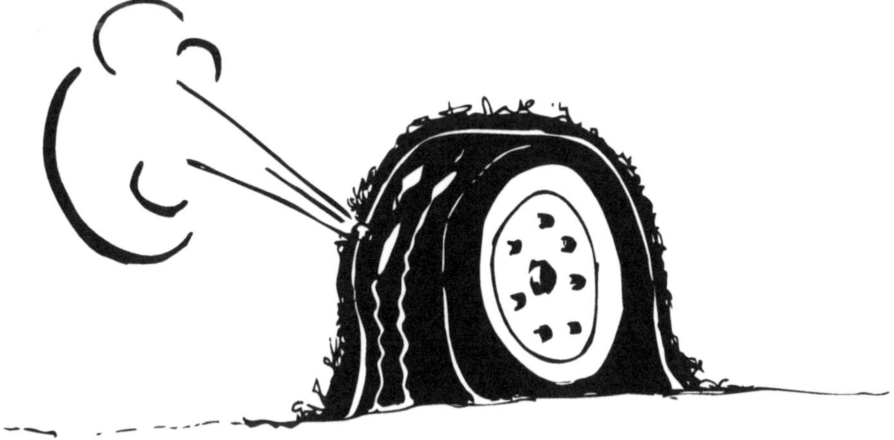

Not fun

It's not fun
without a phone.

Some would rather dial
than live without phone.

It makes no sense—
because if you dial
while you drive,
there won't be any more fun.

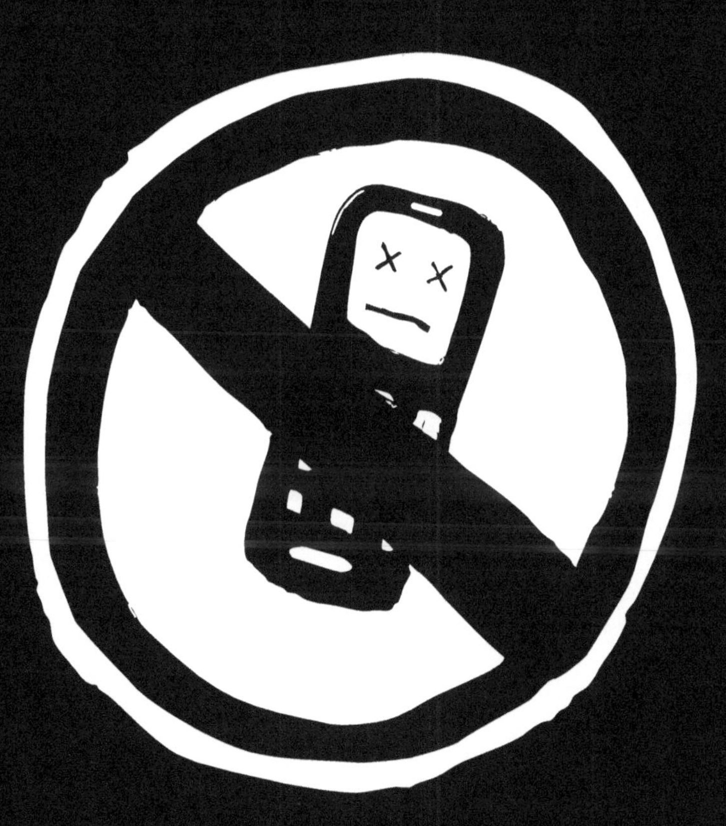

Sweet home

Even if it isn't,
if you *feel* it—
sing it:

Sweet home Alabama!

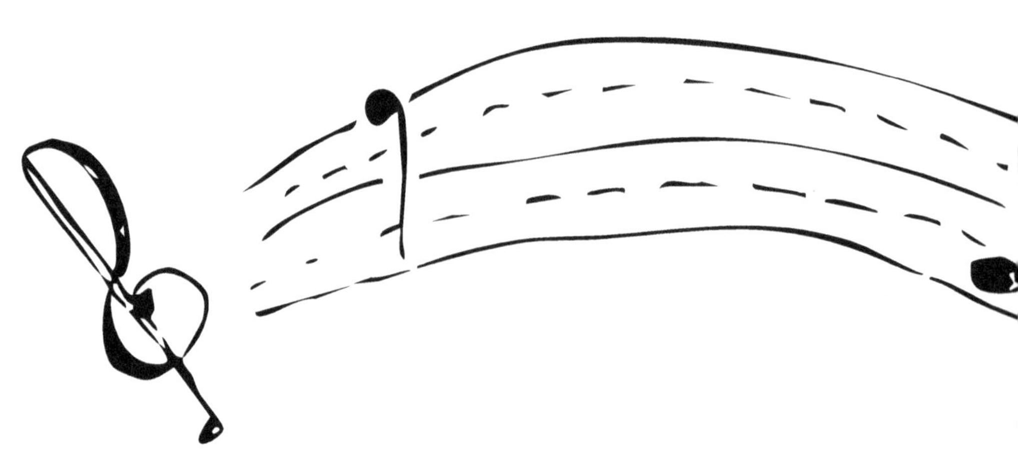

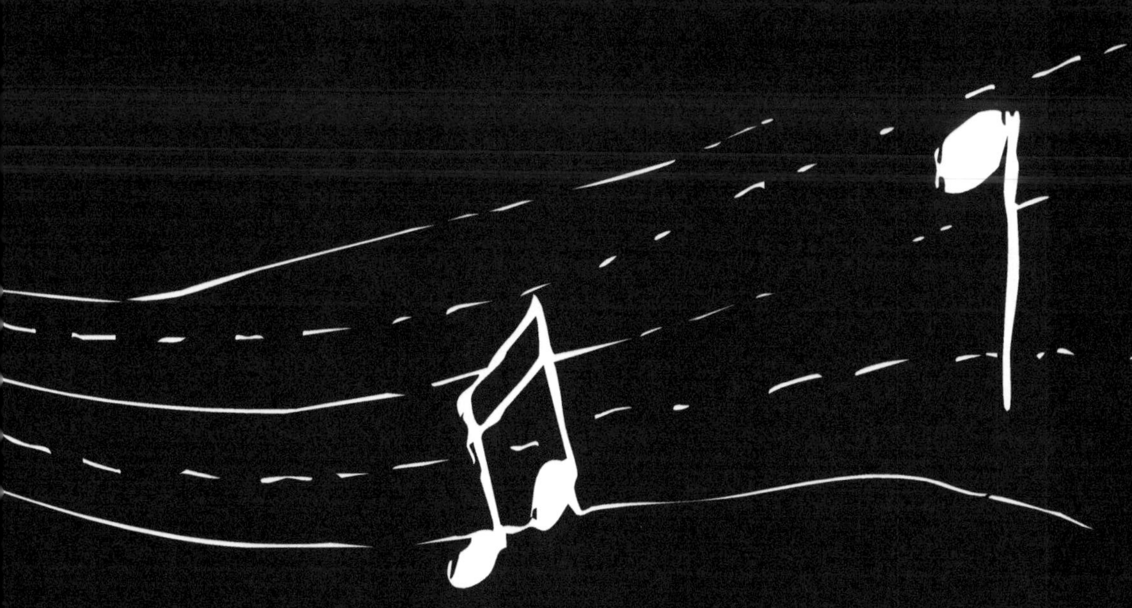
Alabama

Smart decision

Right or left?
Right or left?

Oh my God!
What a difficult decision!

Right or left?
Right or left?

Oh my God!
What a stress!

Right or left?
Right or left?

I think the smartest thing to do is...

Eeny, meeny, miny, moe.

Turns

If you look at the map,
some turns look
like a happy face.

And some turns look
like a mad face.

But if the whole trip
is just one straight line...

It looks like a bored face.

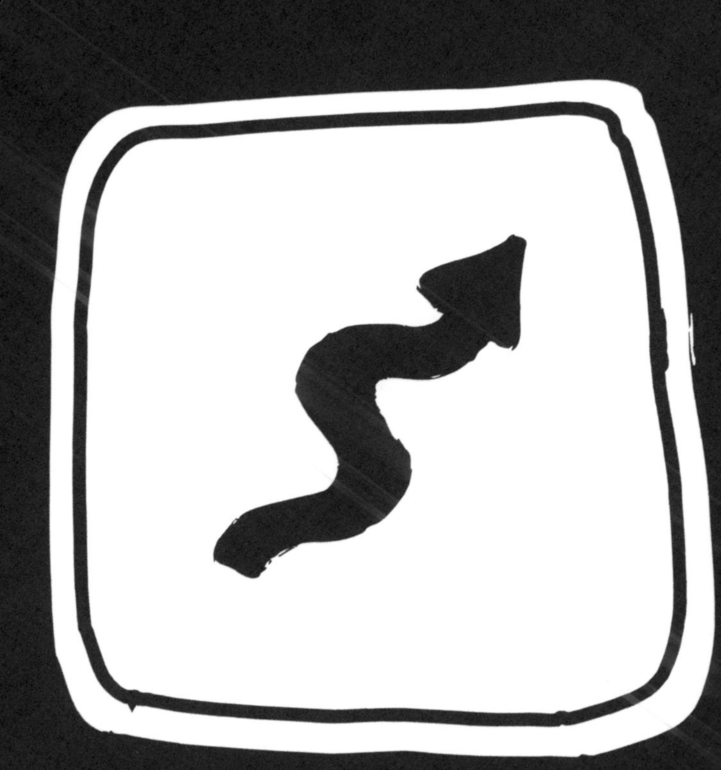

Fall in love

While I'm on the road
I can easily fall in love
in love
with nature...

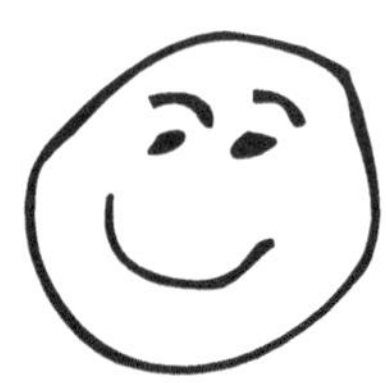

Fall, fall, fall in love with the sunrise.

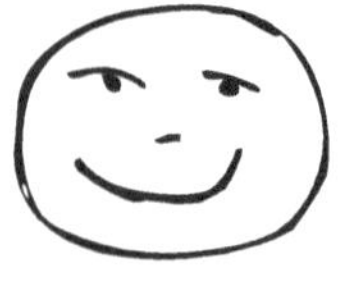

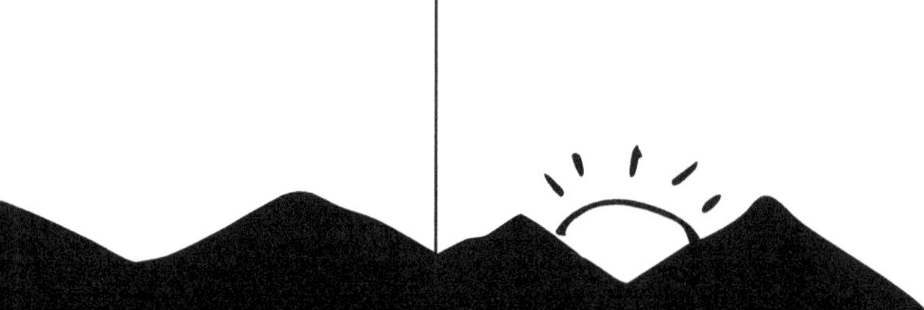

Fall, fall, fall in love with the sunset.

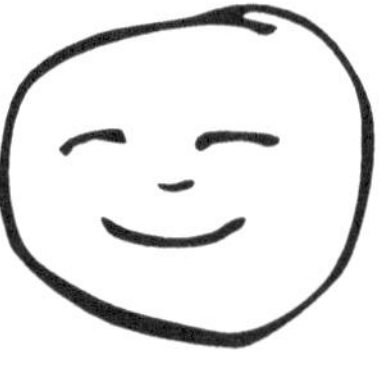

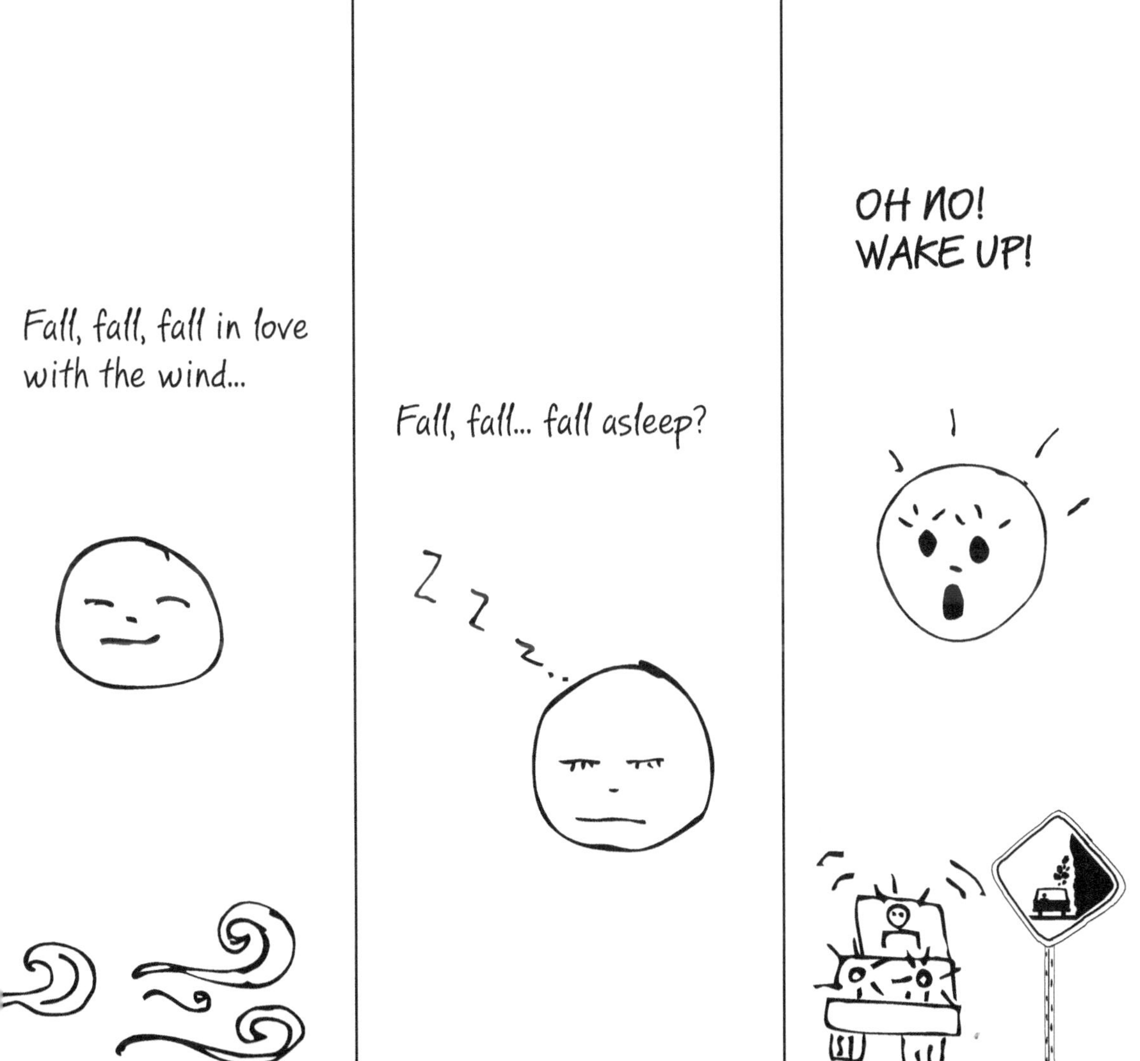
Fall, fall, fall in love with the wind...
Fall, fall... fall asleep?
OH NO!
WAKE UP!

Windflowers

Have you seen a Windflower?

They are like Sunflowers,
but instead of facing the sun
they are facing the wind.

They are so big that they seem to be
planted by giants.

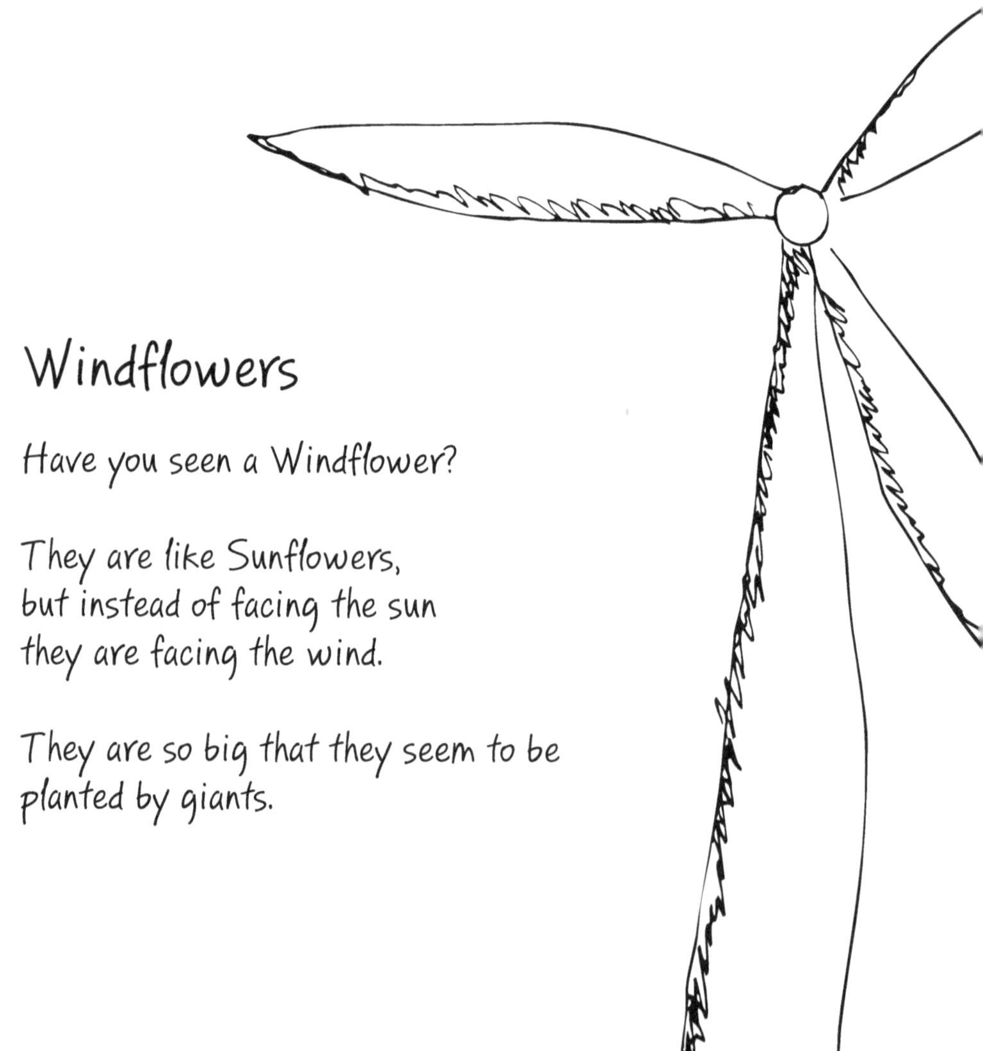

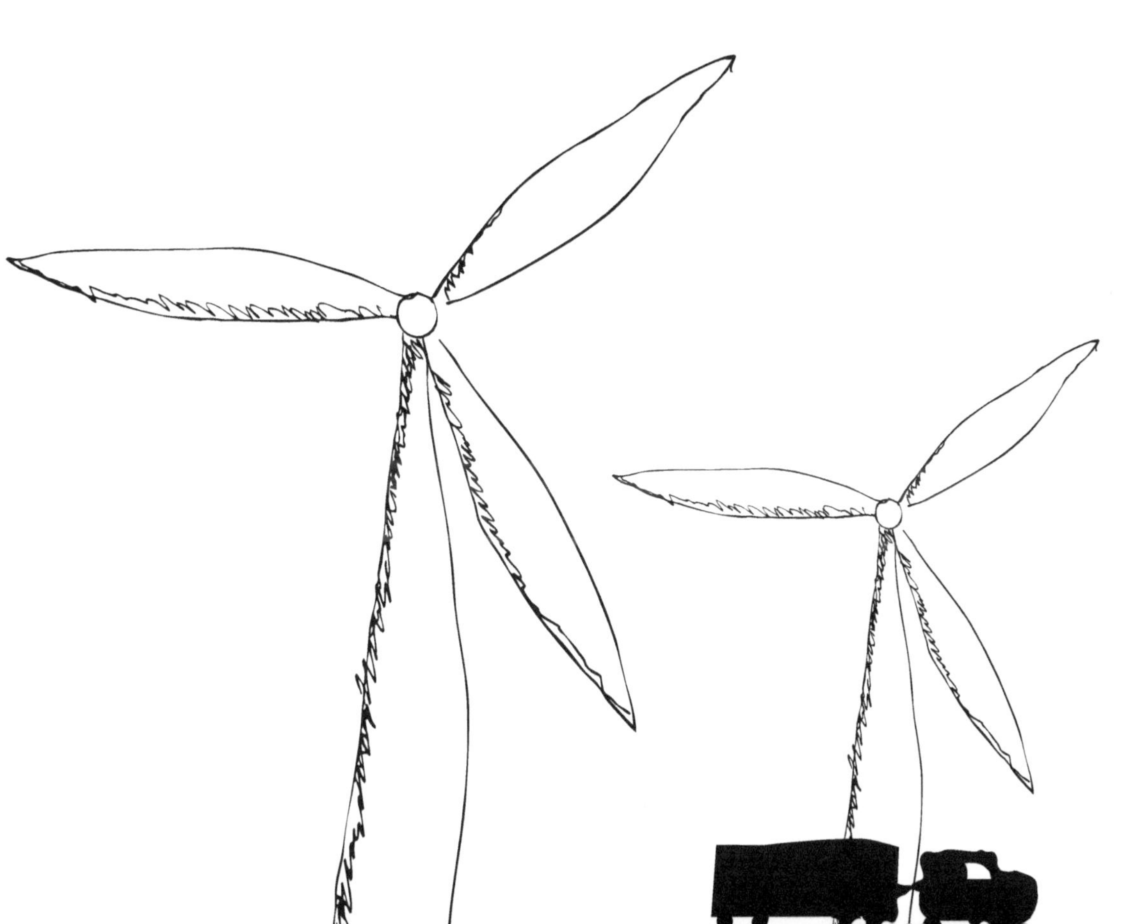

The Smashing Bugs

—Have you seen a smashing?
—No, what's that?
—Oh my God!
Don't tell me you've missed it.
It's trending everywhere—
a collective art movement.
You *have* to see the work;
each one is a masterpiece.
You can really feel
how they died for it.

ART

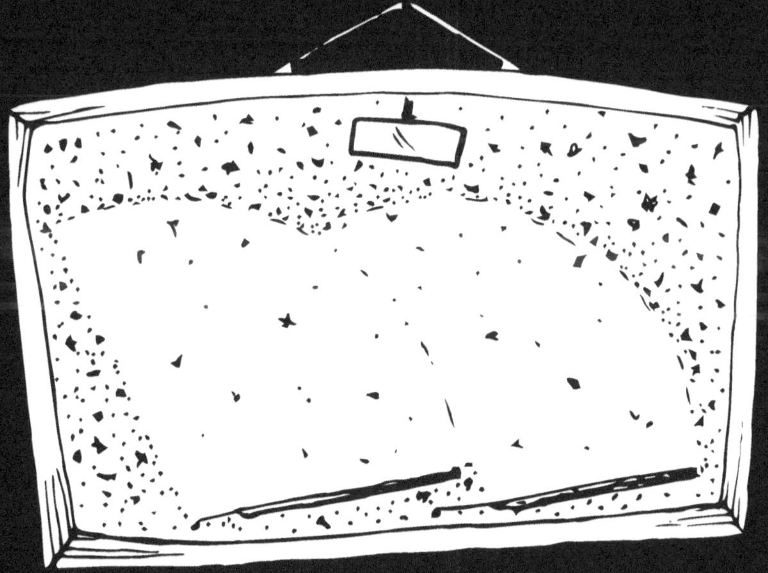

"The rearview mirror here doesn't actually exist in trucks; it is only for reference."

Detour

Why now?
Oh no!
Why, why?

I don't know this new road,
I don't want to get out.
Why, why?
I don't know anything around.
Why, why, why me?

Why not?
Just calm down,
follow the signs,
and enjoy the new road.

Note: It is valid to cry, scream and swear... before you calm down.

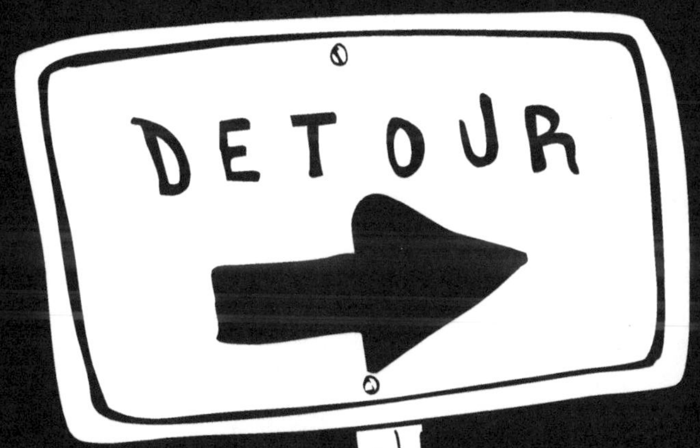
DETOUR

Run, Run!

I'm always running
from here to there
without stopping.

Run, run,
all the time!
Just run and run!
No one can beat me!
Cause I'm the running man!

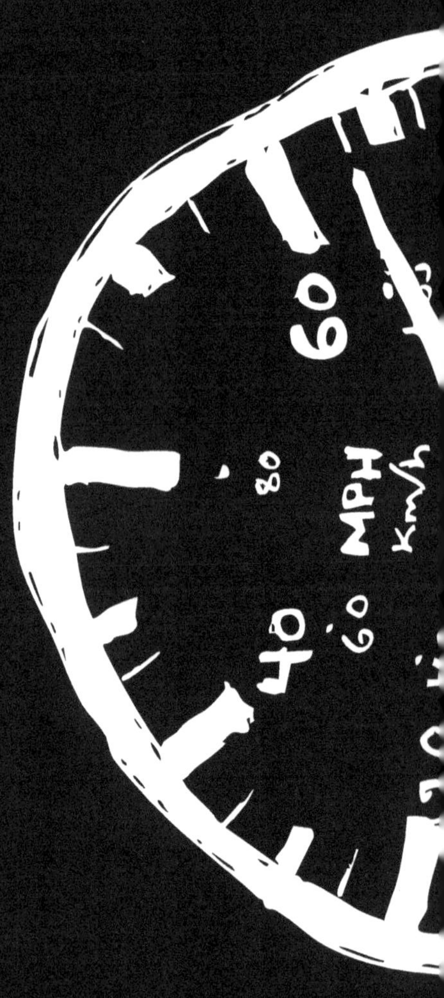

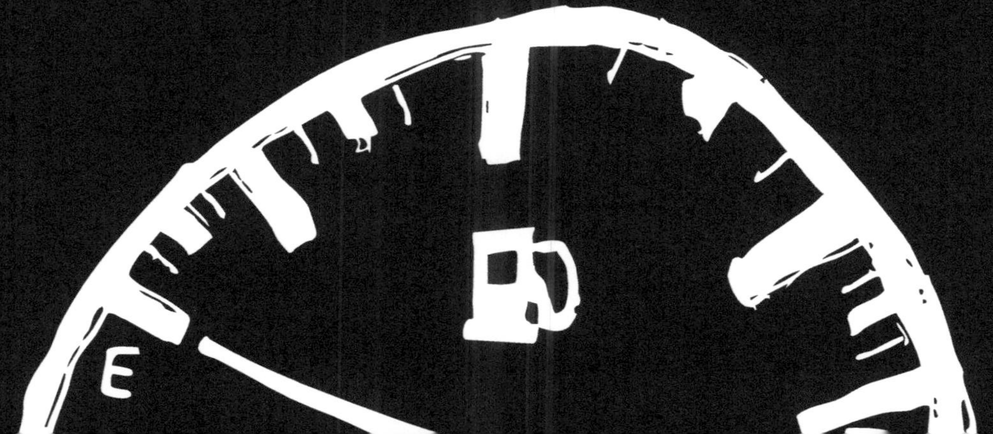

Run, run!
Yes!
Run, run!
Yahoo!
Run, run!

Oops!
I ran out of fuel.

Note: This poem will continue as soon as I walk back from the gas station.

Stop

Sometimes on the road
you have to stop.

But why?
I don't want to.
Neither do I,
nor he,
nor she,
nor they,
nor any of us.

But if we all keep going...
we will all end.

We will all end...
We will all end...
We will all end...
...end.

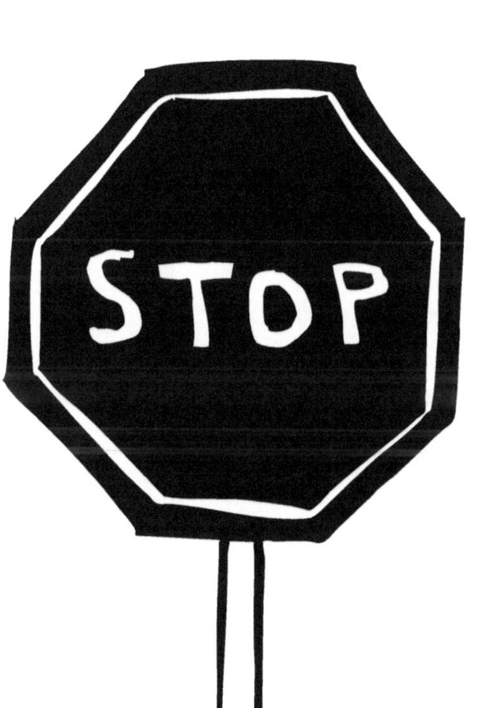
STOP

On time

—Have you ever been on time?

—Where is that?

—It is between
Early and Late.

It's not easy to get there,
but it ain't impossible.

It is a nice place.
I suggest you visit.
I bet you will like it.

Note: I also suggest you park on Early Street. It's better than Late.

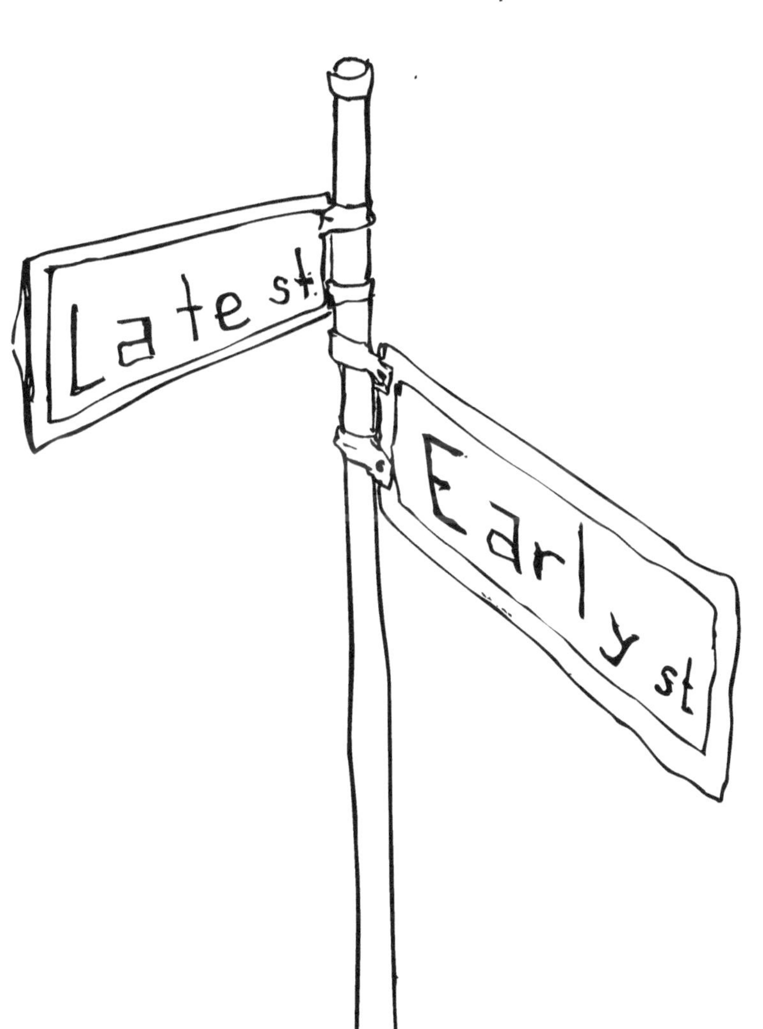

Late st.
Early st.

The round table

Oh, what an exclusive restaurant!
It is so elite
that only one or two people
can get in.

You can eat almost anything;
the best dishes are homemade.
Oh, what exquisiteness!

And the view? It's extravagant.
You can change the scenery physically,
not virtually—
from mountains to lakes,
or from the sea to...

Hold on!
Someone is trying to tell me something.
It's in signs... oh, I get it!
He is suggesting I change my view.
What kindness!

Seriously, this is the best restaurant.

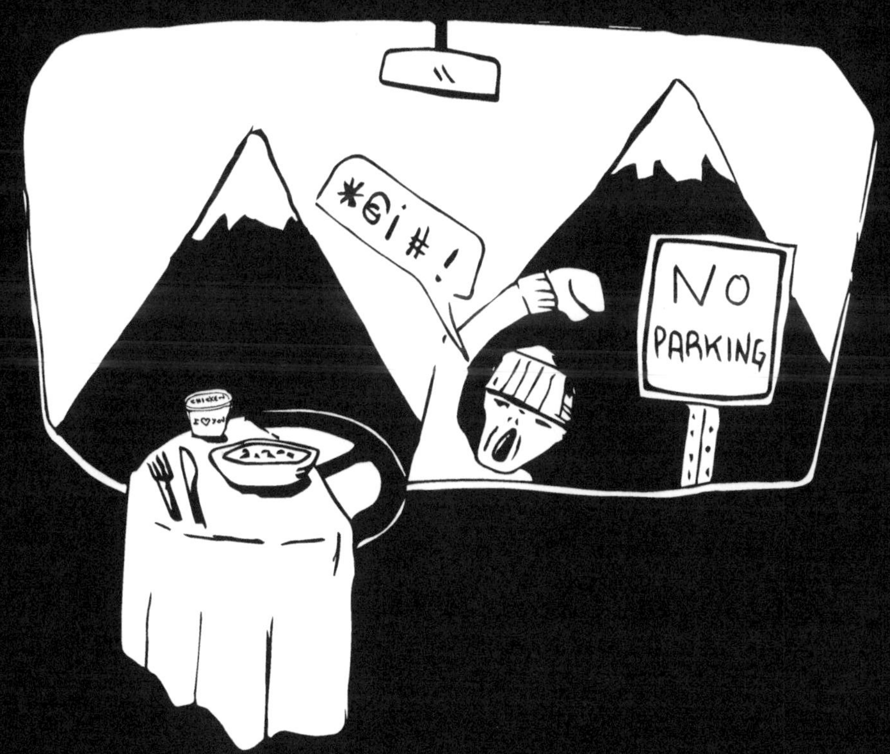

"The rearview mirror here doesn't actually exist in trucks; it is only for reference."

Speed limit

There are some roads
where you can speed like a rabbit,
and some roads
where you must crawl like a turtle.

Just remember to obey the speed limit,
or you might win:

A ticket from the Law,
or a one-way trip
like a smashed bug.

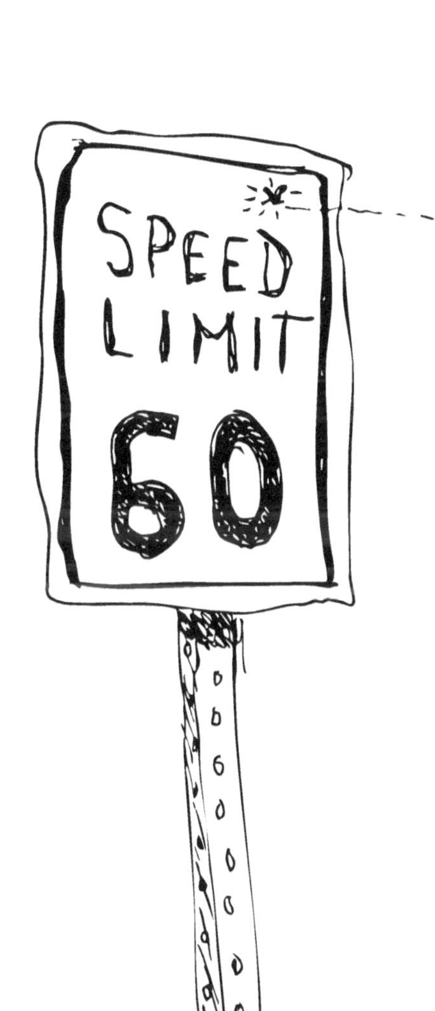

SPEED
LIMIT
60

Restroom

What a delicate topic!
We could write
a thousand words about it.

We could begin with the cleaning...
Uh wow! Such a delicate topic.

Or what about the smell?
Uh wow! Such a delicate topic.

We could even make an encyclopedia
about it.

Or what about the wait to get in?
Uh wow! Such a delicate topic.

You know what? Let me flush first
before I continue
with such a delicate topic.

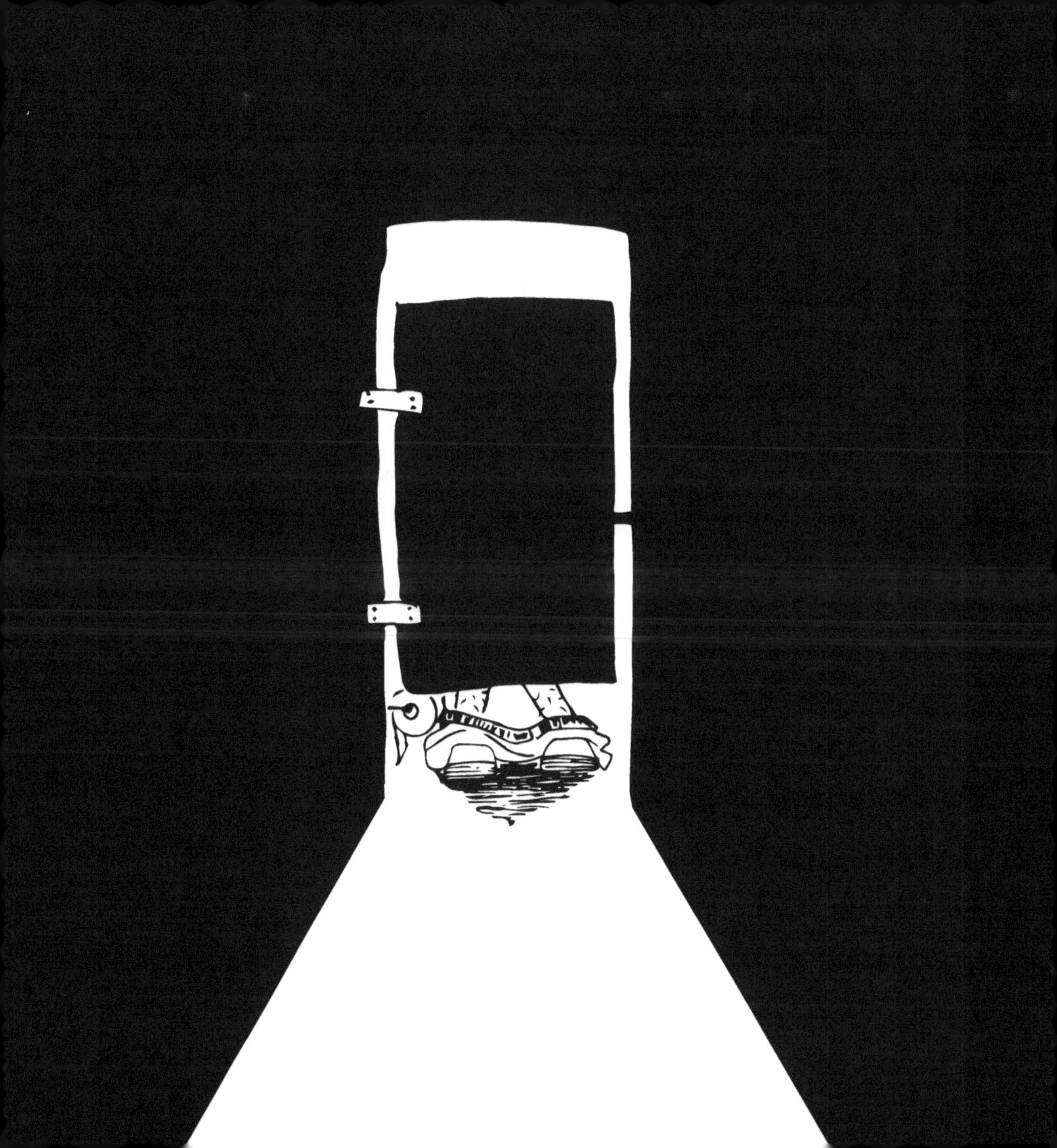

Tic toc

Tic toc, tic toc...
"60 minutes warning"
I'm a little bit stressed.

Tic toc, tic toc...
"30 minutes warning"
I'm a little stressed!

Tic toc, tic toc...
"15 minutes warning"
I'm stressed!!

Tic toc, tic toc...
"5 minutes warning"
AM STRESSED I !!!

Finally, a safe heaven
with three minutes left...
to clean my seat.

8 HR DOT

01:20:03

11 HR DOT

01:20:03

14 HR DOT

00:03:00

70 HR DOT

00:03:00

""Professional drivers follow four different clocks to keep the road safe for everyone.""

Toxic signs

If you see a skull sign
with crossbones:
Be aware.

Keep your distance,
or bring your mask and gloves
to get closer.

Because usually,
what is behind the sign
is so charming...

that you will melt for it.

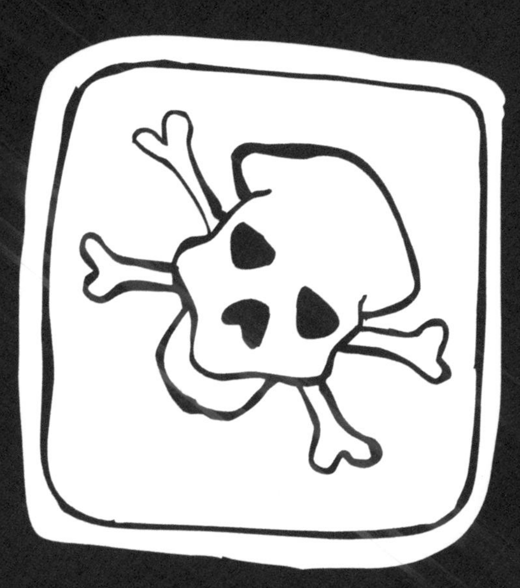

Backing

First, I set up my truck
on my left side.
Then, I turn right
to go left.
Then, I turn left
to go right.

I do my little waves,
then I stop and pull up.
To fix it and start all over—
again and again,

Finally after twenty-two tries.
I did it!
Yeah, yeah, I'm the best.

*"Excuse me, you parked in Dock Seven,
and you're supposed to be in Eleven."*

—What!!!

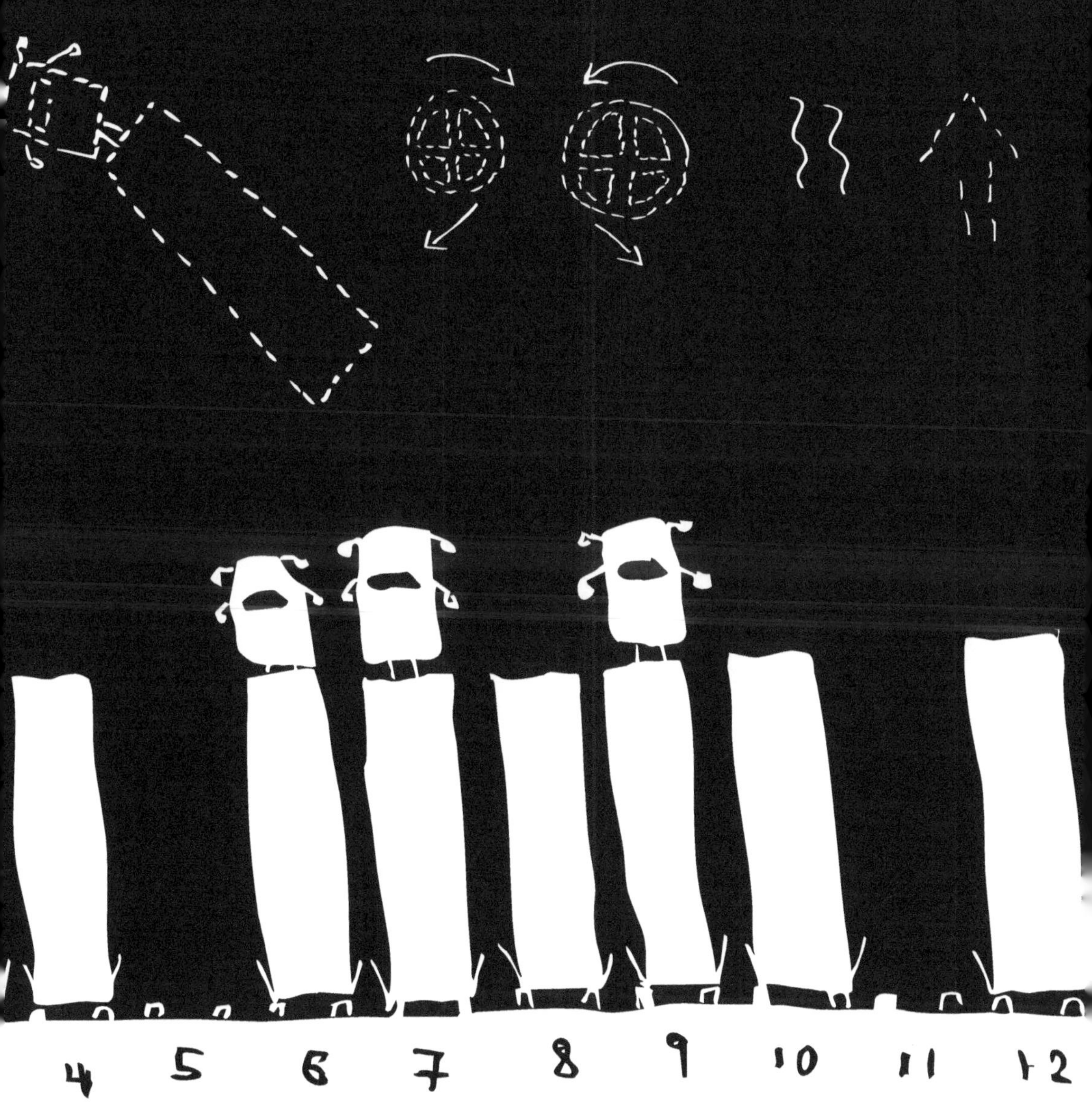

4   5   6   7   8   9   10   11   12

Sleeping alligator

Shhh!
Tiptoe, tiptoe!

If you see an alligator
sleeping in the road,
don't get too close
or it will wake up...

and bite you in the toe!

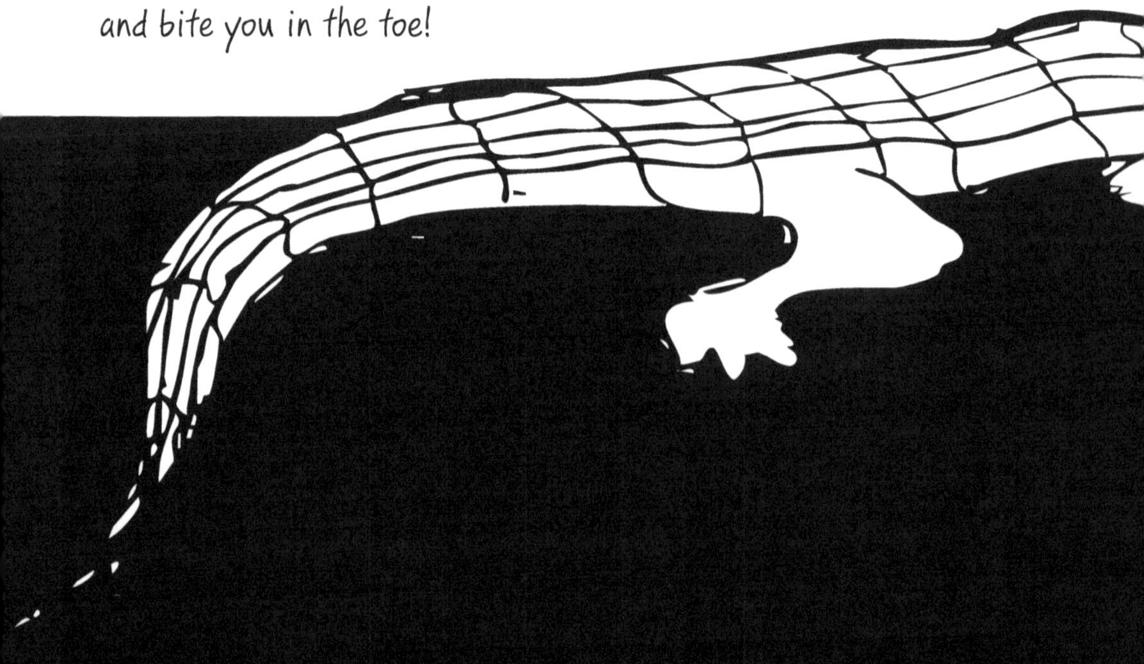

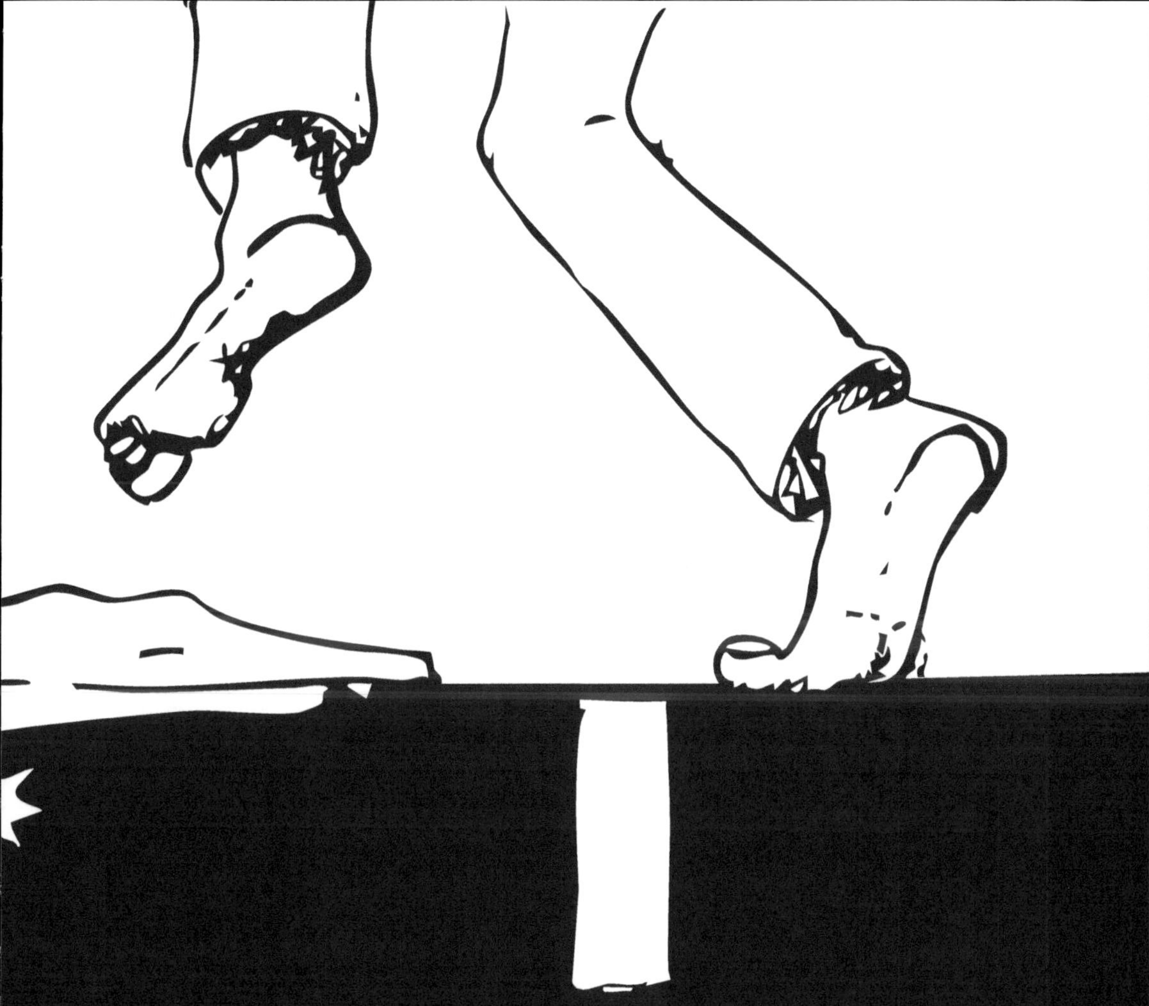

Teams

I like to invent jokes
while I'm driving solo.

I like to tell them
while I'm driving teams.

And I laugh a lot
when I'm driving with Buck...

Cause he is the only one
who gets all of my jokes.

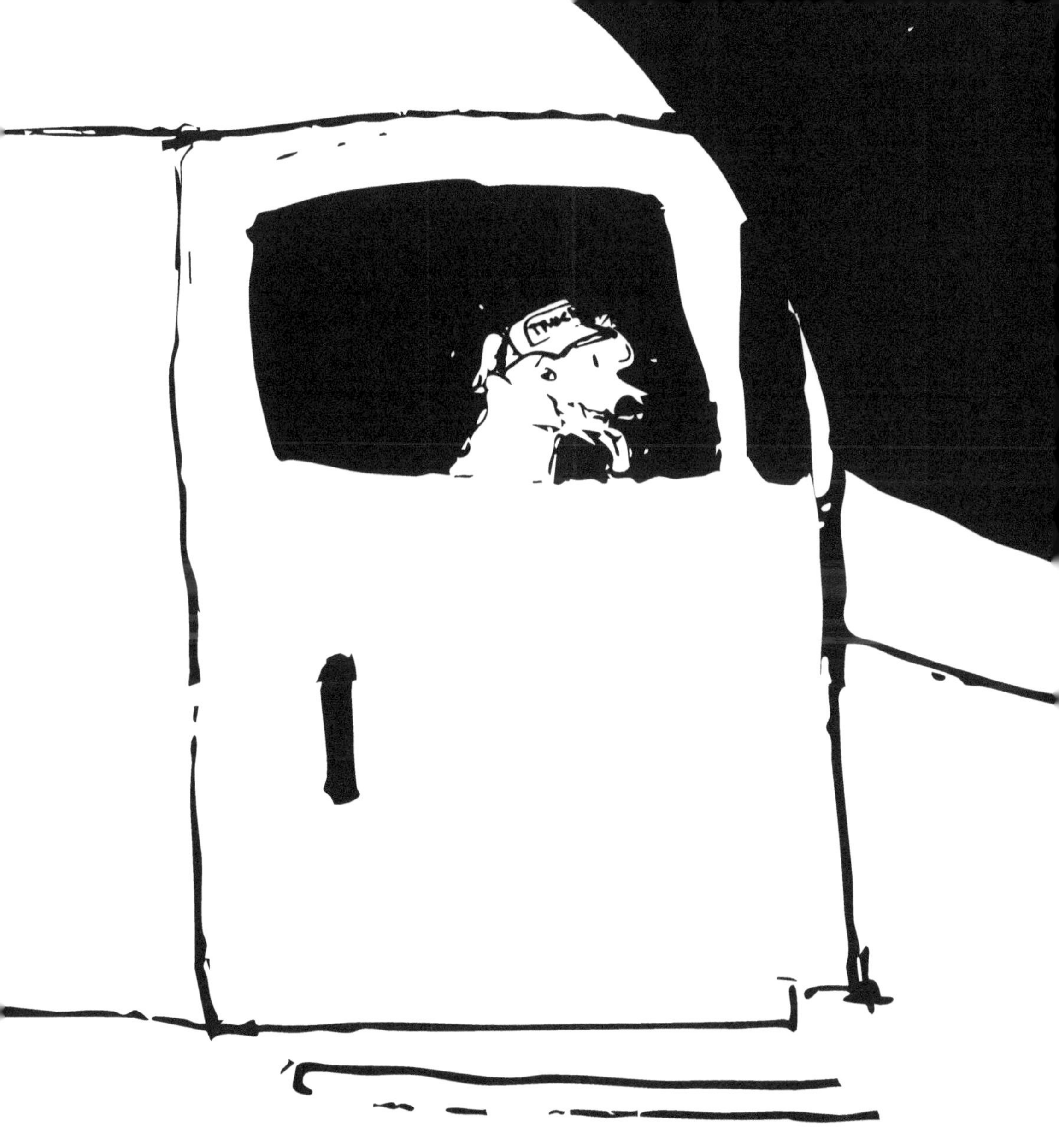

Waiting

What a waste of time—
waiting for someone else
to do their job.

Just wait and wait.
Wait and wait.
Wait and wait.
Wait and wait.
Wait and wait...

Wait a minute!
I can read a book meanwhile.

Okay, don't worry.
I'll wait.

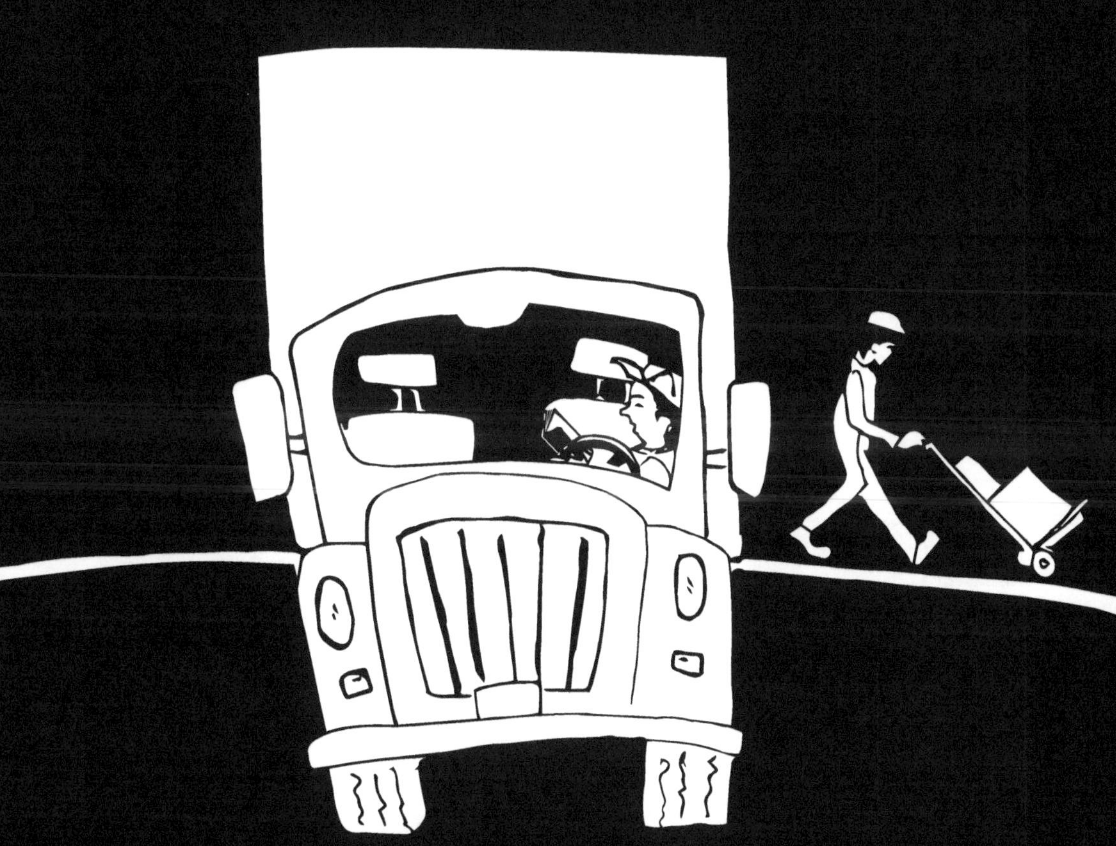

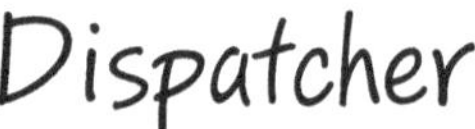

Dispatcher

"Could you deliver
this, this, and this?

And also
this, this, and this?

And I see that you have time
for this, this, and this..."

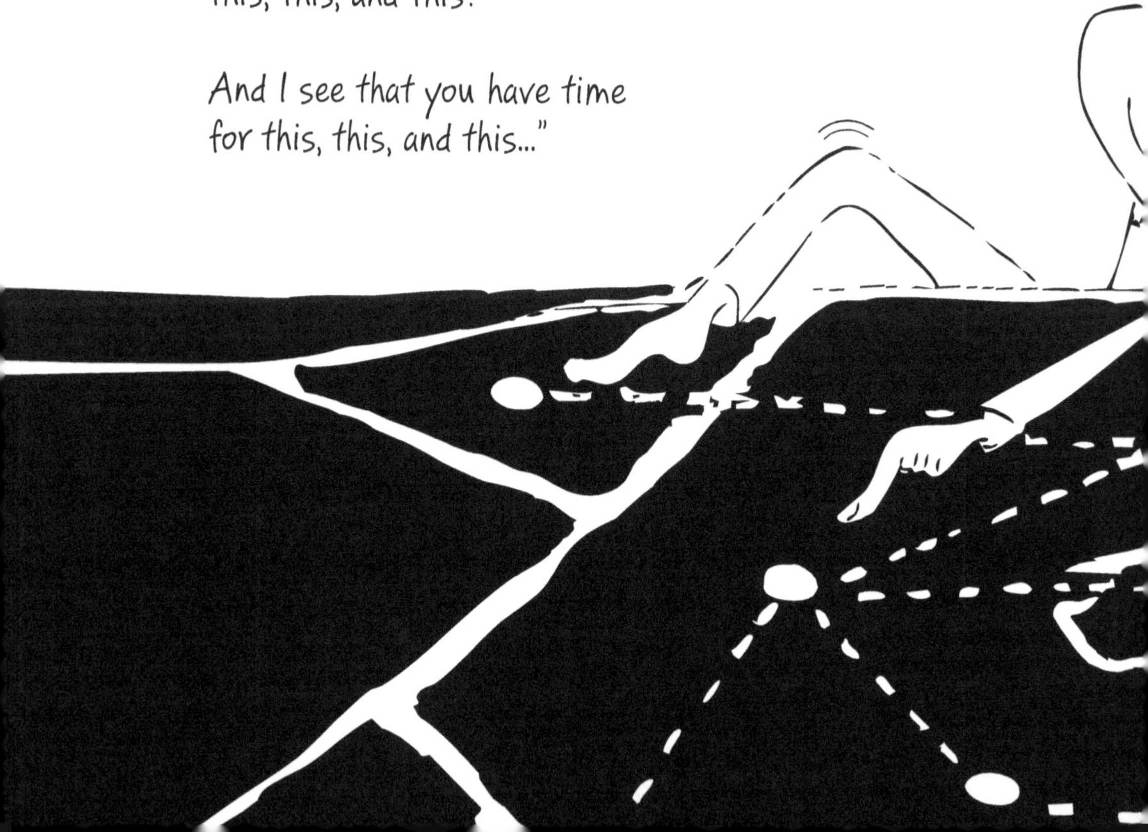

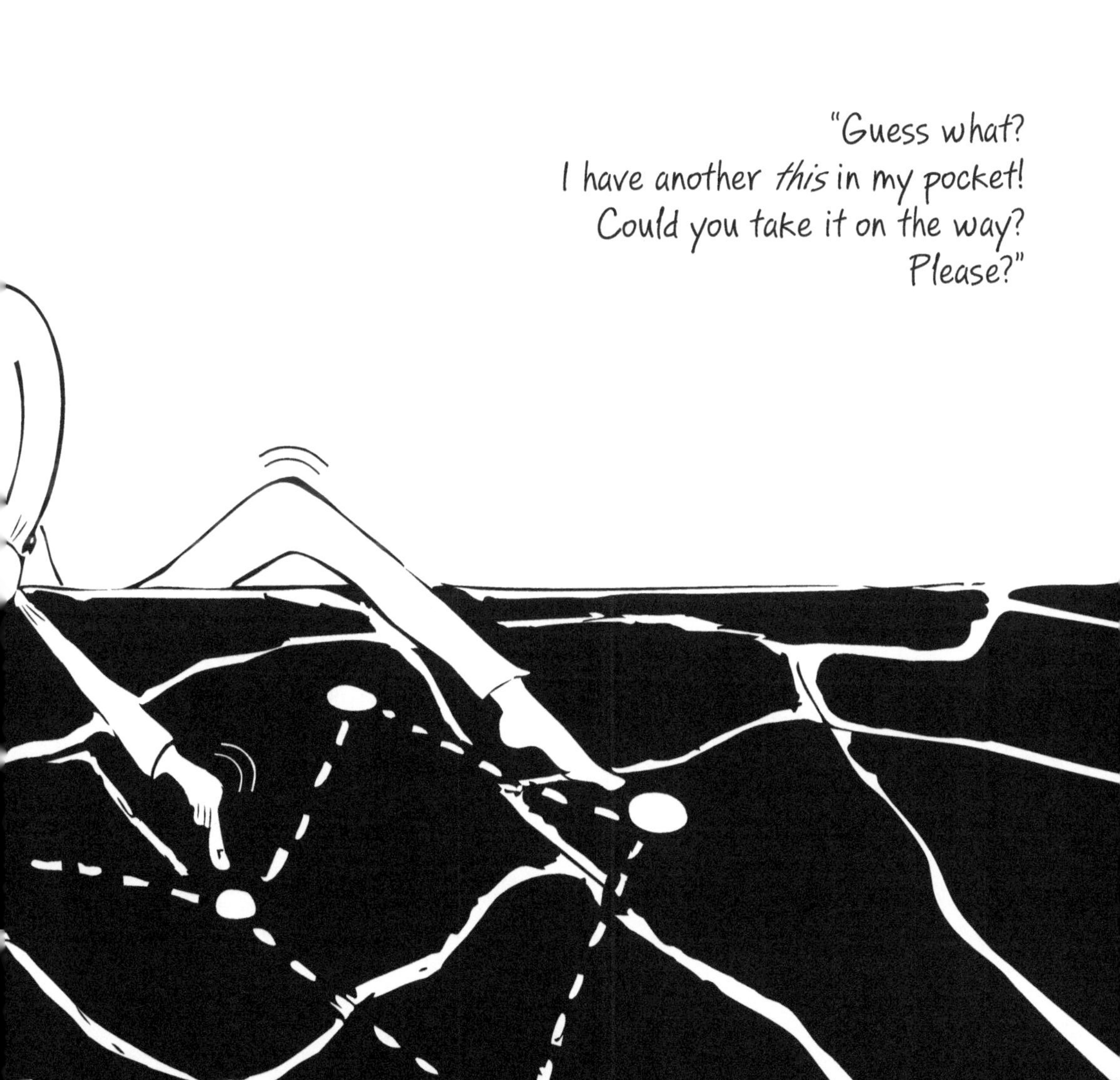
"Guess what?
I have another *this* in my pocket!
Could you take it on the way?
Please?"

Truck signs

What a relief to see
a truck sign without a crossed line!
It means...
you keep rolling.

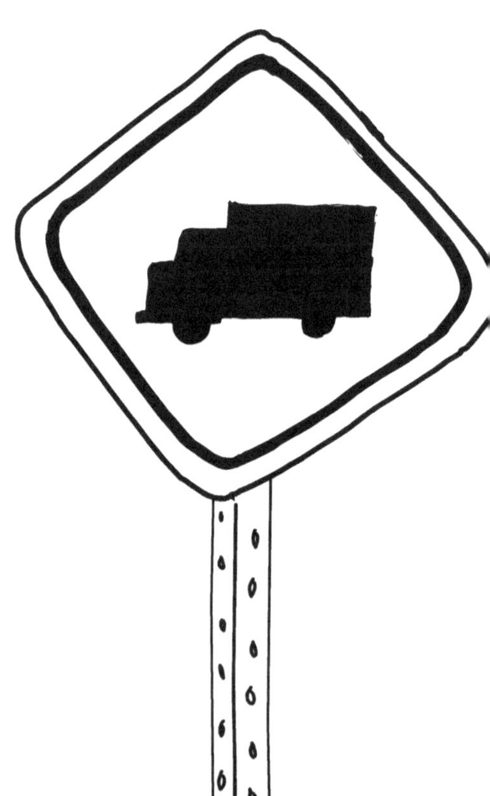

But if it is
a truck sign with a crossed line...

It means...
it means...
what it
really means:

A pain in the... !

Note: You can say "back" at the end.

Billboard

—Car accident?
You better call me!

—Ok.

—No fees
until you win.

—Perfect, because I hit you.

—In that case...
In that case...
In that case...
I think you should call the next billboard!

Note: Did you think you could get rid of the lawyer billboards that easily? We are even in this book!

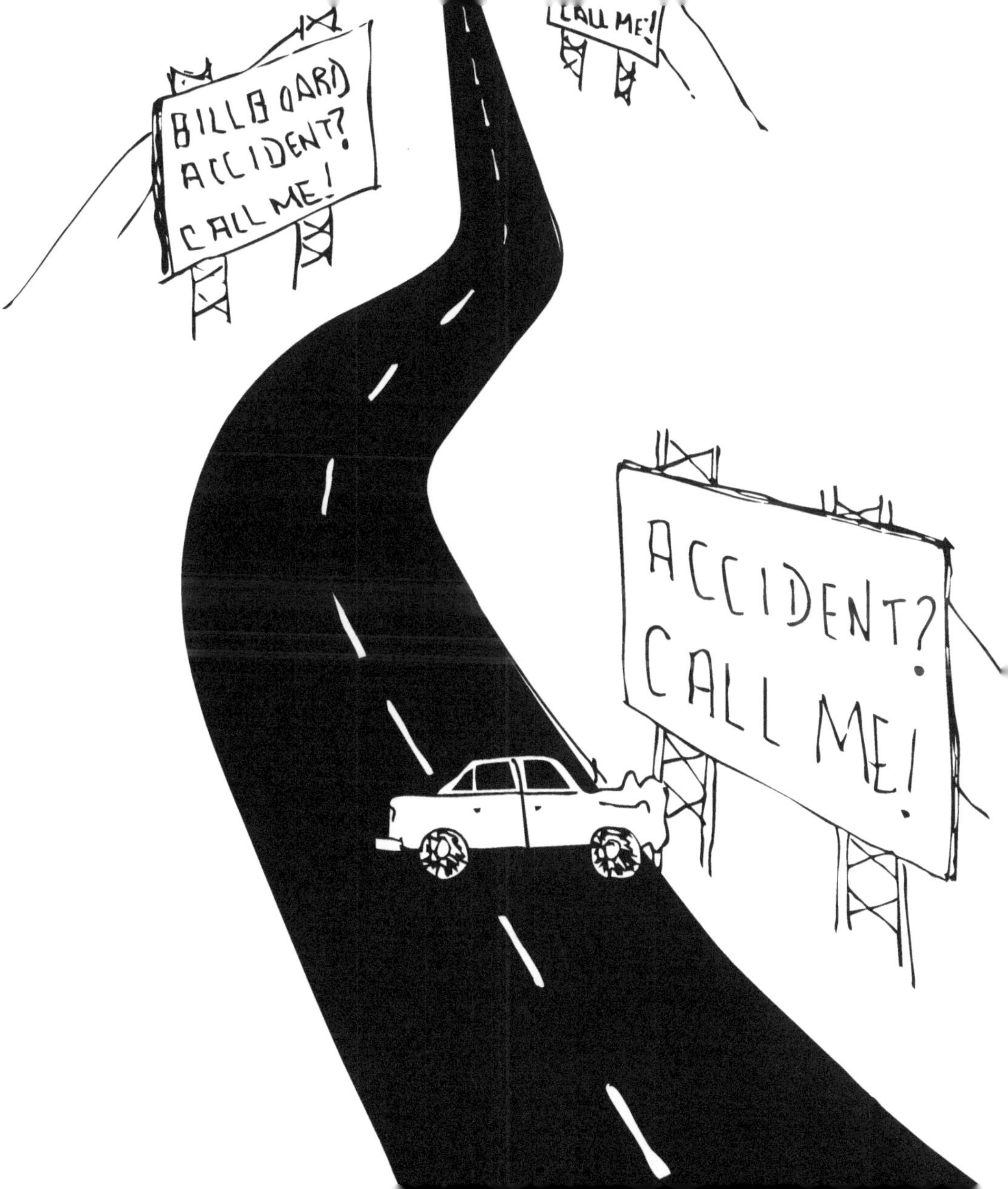

BILLBOARD
ACCIDENT?
CALL ME!
CALL ME!
ACCIDENT?
CALL ME!

Until the end

...keep
and keep
and keep
and keep
and keep
and keep
and keep
and keep
and keep
and keep

working on it
until the end.

It is a peaceful feeling
once you are done!

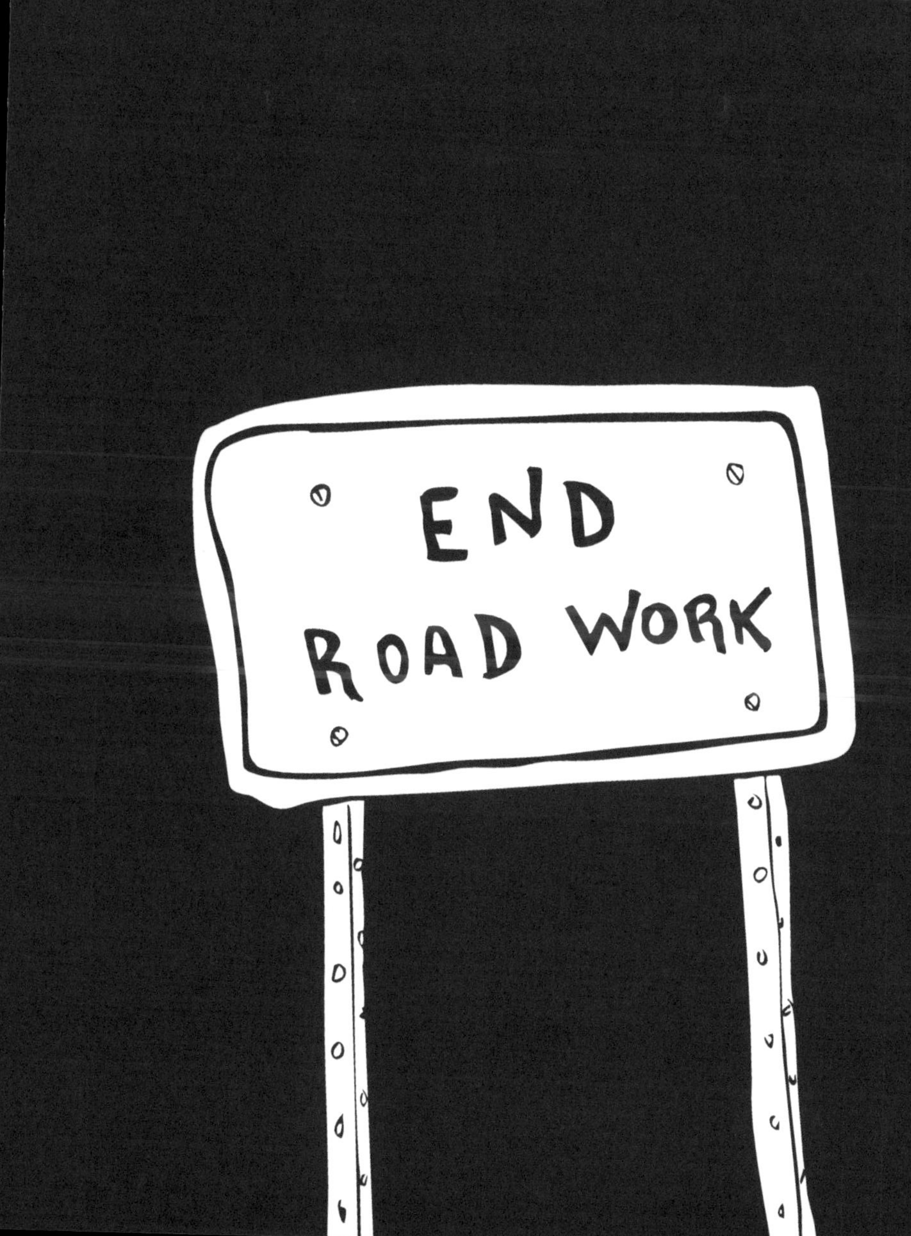

END
ROAD WORK

Dear Truck,

Thanks for bringing
water, food, and supplies
to my house.

And also for bringing this book
to laugh some,
and for bringing my big-belly daddy
safely back home.

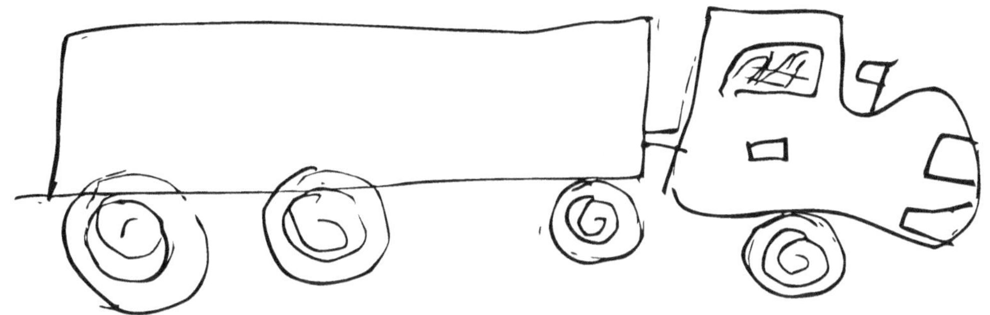

Index

Begin a work 4
Dear deer 6
Flat tire 8
Not fun 10
Sweet home 12
Smart decision 14
Turns 16
Fall in love 18
Windflowers 20
The Smashing Bugs 22
Detour 24
Run, run! 26
Stop 28

On time 30
The round table 32
Speed limit 34
Restroom 36
Tic toc 38
Toxic signs 40
Backing 42
Sleeping alligator 44
Teams 46
Waiting 48
Dispatcher 50
Truck signs 52
Billboard 54
Until the end 56
Dear Truck, 58

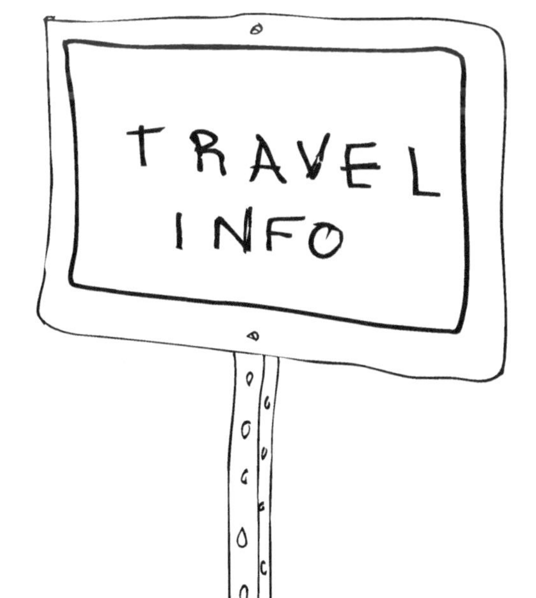

TRAVEL
INFO

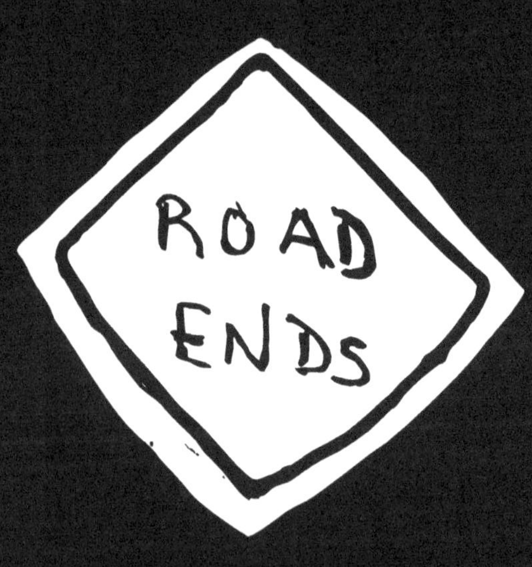
ROAD
ENDS

www.ingramcontent.com/pod-product-compliance
Lightning Source LLC
Chambersburg PA
CBHW042051030726
47599CB00019B/2447